GO TO THE TOP

leave the crowd behind

A DISCIPLESHIP COURSE BASED ON THE BIBLE AND DEGARMO & KEY LYRICS

Light Force

FROM GOSPEL LIGHT

© Copyright 1991 by Eddie DeGarmo and Dana Key.
Registered by Gospel Light, Ventura, CA 93006.
All rights reserved. Printed in the U.S.A.

EDITORIAL STAFF

Mark Maddox, Publisher
Gary S. Greig, Ph.D. Senior Editor
Annette Parrish, Editor
Judith Roth, Writer

SPECIAL ACKNOWLEDGMENTS

Inspired by the lyrics of
Eddie DeGarmo and Dana Key
Developed from a concept by
Robert Michaels
Album Producer, Ron W. Griffin

DESIGN

Ted Killian, Senior Designer

Scripture quotations in this book are from the Holy Bible, *New International Version*, 1973, 1978, 1984 International Bible Society. Used by permission of Zondervan Bible Publishers.

Words and music by Eddie DeGarmo and Dana Key. Copyright © DKB Music/ASCAP, a division of Forefront Communications Group, Inc., 7106 Moores Lane, Suite 200, Brentwood, TN 37027. International copyright secured. All rights reserved. Used by permission.

HOW TO MAKE CLEAN COPIES FROM THIS BOOK

You may make copies of portions of this book with a clean conscience if:

- you (or someone in your organization) are the original purchaser.
- you are using the copies you make for a noncommercial purpose (such as teaching or promoting a ministry) within your church or organization.
- You follow the instructions provided in this book.

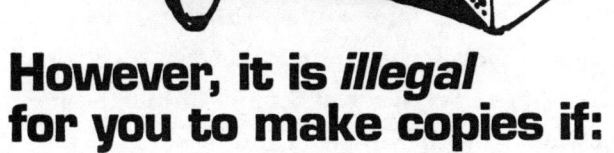

However, it is *illegal* for you to make copies if:

- you are using the material to promote, advertise or sell a product or service other than for ministry fund-raising.
- you are using the material in or on a product for sale.
- you or your organization are not the original purchaser of this book.

By following these guidelines you help us keep our products affordable.

Thank you.
Gospel Light

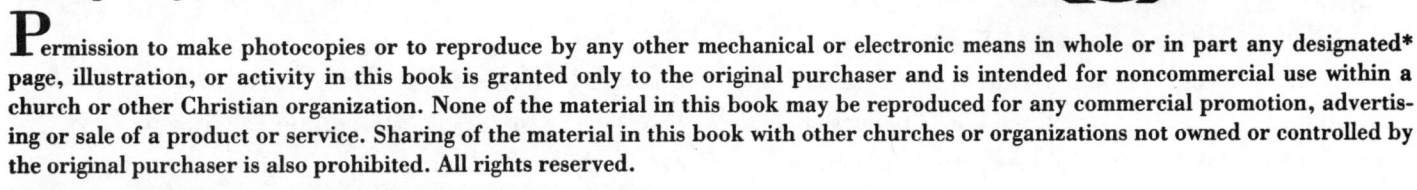

Permission to make photocopies or to reproduce by any other mechanical or electronic means in whole or in part any designated* page, illustration, or activity in this book is granted only to the original purchaser and is intended for noncommercial use within a church or other Christian organization. None of the material in this book may be reproduced for any commercial promotion, advertising or sale of a product or service. Sharing of the material in this book with other churches or organizations not owned or controlled by the original purchaser is also prohibited. All rights reserved.

*Pages with the following notations can be legally reproduced:
© 1991 DKB Music/ASCAP. Allrights reserved. Used by permission. Permission to photocopy granted.
© 1991 DeGarmo and Key by Gospel Light. All rights reserved. Permission to photocopy granted.

TABLE OF CONTENTS

Preface: An Open Letter
from DeGarmo and Key 5
How to Use This Course 6
Tips and Tools
for Studying the Bible 7
Lyrics for the Living God 9
The role of music and song in worship

STEP 1
TAKE THE PLEDGE 10
The decision to follow Jesus; the problem of sin; repentance; surrendering; public confession.

STEP 2
READ THE WORD 19
What is Scripture?; the authority of Scripture; basic contents and purpose; the Christian discipline of Bible study; meditating on the Word; hearing the Bible taught.

Talk Sheet
THE PROCESS OF BIBLE STUDY 31
Personal preparation; methods; tools.

STEP 3
GO TO THE TOP 33
What is prayer?; total access to God; the Christian discipline of prayer; the role of the Holy Spirit; creatures created to communicate with the Creator; purpose of prayer; Jesus' example; types of prayers.

Talk Sheet
DEVELOPING A PRAYER LIFE 45
Proper attitudes; regularity; hindrances to prayer; how to pray—mode, posture, private and group prayer, prayer partners; effects of prayer.

STEP 4
ULTIMATE RULER 47
Recognizing your position in Christ; illustration of vine and branches; bearing fruit; the Lord "prunes" believers to increase their fruitfulness; getting rid of dead branches (sin); giving up things for Christ; types of fruit.

Talk Sheet
THE FRUIT OF THE SPIRIT 57
Galatians 5:22,23; "attitude" spiritual fruit; right actions follow right attitudes; contrasting the acts of sinful nature with the fruit of the Spirit.

STEP 5
FAMILY REUNION 59
Living at peace with other believers; living in fellowship; the Church; accountability; training; caring for each other; worshiping together.

Talk Sheet
SPIRITUAL GIFTS 69
What are spiritual gifts?; Holy Spirit as the source; different gifts, one Spirit; purpose of gifts; identify and plan to use your gifts.

STEP 6
STAND, FIGHT, WIN 71
Understanding temptation and spiritual warfare; God provides tools for the battle; the armor of God; the costs and rewards of discipleship; handling failure; when a brother or sister fails.

Talk Sheet
SHINING AS STARS 81
Christians in society; Christian responsibility; help the poor, protect the innocent; practical Christian activism.

STEP 7
THE REST OF MY LIFE 83
Making Jesus Lord of every area of your life; being God's hands and feet; serving Christ by serving others; vocation and avocation; making disciples.

Talk Sheet
YOUR PERSONAL TESTIMONY 93
What's a witness?; the command to witness; you are competent to witness; preparing your personal testimony.

AN OPEN LETTER FROM DEGARMO & KEY

We as DeGarmo and Key have been making music for over a decade. In just a short period of time we have seen a lot of things come and go. And, we've seen how these changes affect the young people we work with in the church.

We live in a trendy world. What is fashionable for one to think and do today is gone tomorrow. In a world where culture is constantly changing and bombarding us with pressure to change with it, it is really difficult for any of us to find consistency. The only sure guidepost is God's Word.

When we began performing as DeGarmo and Key, our goals were very simple. We wanted our music to be used as a tool to help others have a closer walk with Jesus. We do hope people really enjoy our music, but we know that it takes more than music to make a real difference in someone's life. It takes a steady diet of God's Word.

Through the years we have often enclosed Bible studies with many of our records and videos. Two years ago, in response to a report from Barna Research Group indicating biblical literacy at an all-time low, we launched *The Pledge* tour—an eighteen-month effort to promote Bible reading, sponsored by *The NIV Student Bible*.

Now, with *Go to the Top*, we are extremely happy to be able to present a full-fledged Bible curriculum. In a way, we hope to become "silent partners" with you as you lead the young people in your group through the *Go to the Top* discipleship study.

The title *Go to the Top* comes from the theme of a believer, "Going to the top to get things done." "The top," of course, is being at the throne of grace with God the Father and His Son, Jesus. That's the place where our resources lie—the place where we learn to live to honor Him and get the strength to make it through this life.

It is our hope that this study will help you and the members of your group grow closer to Jesus. May He bless your ministry.

Eddie DeGarmo and Dana Key

HOW TO USE THIS COURSE

Although the lesson plans in this course are fairly self-explanatory, taking the time to read this brief article may increase the effectiveness of your teaching.

Music
Go to the Top is a discipleship course that uses music by DeGarmo and Key to communicate to young adults. The first session, Step 1—Take the Pledge uses the song "The Pledge" from the album *The Pledge*. Subsequent sessions use music from the *Go to the Top* album.

It's been said that music calms the hearts of wild beasts. While that may be an overstatement, it certainly is true that music communicates on a deep level. That's why we suggest that you get the albums suggested for use in this study. Although not required in order to teach the course, using the music where suggested in the lesson plans will grab students' interest, add another dimension to the lesson and will increase students' retention of learning.

Seven to Thirteen Sessions
The study is built around seven steps to being a committed disciple. These seven steps are the topics of the seven basic lessons. If you would like a full quarter of lessons (13) or if you would like to teach a midweek or evening study that is correlated to the seven basic lessons, there are six additional, optional lesson outlines and worksheets provided. We've called these optional sessions **"Talk Sheets"** since one tear-out sheet has an outline for the "talk" or session and a reproducible worksheet/handout. Turn to the Table of Contents to see how the Talk Sheets correlate to the seven basic sessions (The first optional session, "The Process of Bible Study," follows "Step 2—Read the Word.").

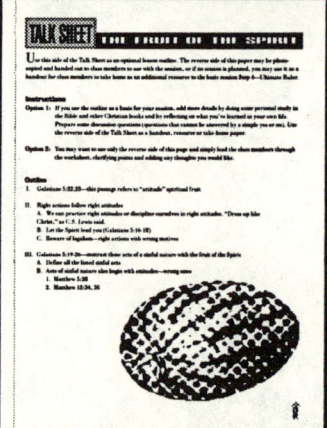

Basic Lesson Format
The song lyrics by DeGarmo and Key appear twice in each of the seven basic sessions—once at the beginning of each lesson to introduce that week's theme and again at the end of each session as a **reproducible lyric sheet.**

Each session has an **introductory section for the leader**. This section gives the lesson theme, Bible memory verse and a checklist that will help the leader know when the class has accomplished the purpose of the session.

The lesson plan gives **ideas for conducting the session** including suggested wording for discussion questions. In each session there are many **optional activities**. You may choose not to use the optional lesson activities. If this is your choice, your lesson will be built around Bible reading and discussion. This is a classic teaching method and it may work well for you. However, choosing to use some or all of the creative optional activities will put a little spark into the course, especially if your students are younger teenagers.

Following the lesson plan you will find a reproducible student handout referred to in the course as the **Self-Evaluation Sheet**. Tear this page out and photocopy it, one for each class member. (You may want to have a couple of extras on hand for visitors.) The Self-Evaluation Sheet is given to students at the end of each basic session for students to work on at home. The sheet features the **Bible Memory Verse, Personal Evaluation Quiz** and **Personal Journal**.

Adapting for Younger Teenagers

If your students are younger than juniors in high school you may need to adapt some of the sessions. This is easily accomplished by choosing to use more of the creative optional activities (to hold their interest) and by simplifying the language of some of the discussion questions. The course was designed to be flexible. Although written for young adults (juniors in high school to sophomores in college), younger students were also kept in mind.

Glance through the course to get an overall idea of how it works. Then relax and enjoy it! Leading a class through the material will be an experience of learning and stretching for all involved. We at Gospel Light hope it will also be a very rewarding experience for you.

Tips & Tools FOR STUDYING THE BIBLE

The Bible is a formidable book. It is long. It is complex. And it is holy. But God did not intend for it to be unread—even if we think it is intellectually threatening. It is His open letter to us. Sometimes it is a love letter and sometimes it is a letter of reprimand, but always it is a letter that is to be read and understood.

Understanding the Bible can be accomplished immediately upon reading it and it can be the goal of a lifetime. For, as we mature as Christians, new depths and meanings are uncovered. This keeps the Bible interesting.

Scholars have spent their lives studying this one book. So it is pretty presumptuous of people who have grown up in church and Sunday School to assume that they no longer need to read the Word because they've read or "heard it all."

If all of this sounds confusing, don't worry. There are a few simple tips and tools that can help you get more from your reading of the Word and that will enrich your Bible study.

TIPS

Plan. Set aside a time to read the Bible. A time every day is optimal. But if that is not realistic, commit to three days a week, or five. If you cannot avoid missing your Bible study time, try to reschedule it. Don't feel defeated and quit.

It is also important to have a quiet place where you can go to read and meditate and not be disturbed.

Think about what you want to read: one of the Gospels? the letters of Paul? Perhaps you would like to study a Bible personality such as David or a theme such as redemption. Consider the areas of your life where you need to grow or think of an area where you need to increase your understanding. Then personalize your study to meet the needs you've identified.

Prepare. Before you begin your study, examine your thoughts. Is there any distraction or worry that you need to attend to before your study? Do you need to apologize to someone for being cross? Do you need to confess to God a sin that is burdening your heart?

Pray. Ask God to open your "spiritual eyes" to His Word.

TOOLS

A few resources can help greatly in your understanding of the Bible. These tools are especially useful when you come across passages that are difficult for you to understand. Here is a list of some of the resources you may want to acquire or have available for the students in your group. A visit to a Christian bookstore or the library of a Christian college or seminary will familiarize you with many of them.

Concordances—Give locations in the Bible where certain words are used. This is helpful if you are researching topics such as "the temple" or if you are trying to locate a familiar verse but only know a word or two of its content.

Bible Dictionaries—Define words and terms as they are used in Scripture.

Topical Indexes—Give numerous references of where passages using certain words or concerning certain topics can be found.

Commentaries—Explain the meaning of Scripture. Commentaries often clarify the meaning of the original language of the Bible text (usually Hebrew or Greek but in a few places Aramaic). They may also explain ancient traditions or cultural settings in order to help the reader understand the full meaning of a passage. Commentaries can be scholarly or simple. We recommend the classic *What the Bible Is All About* by Henrietta Mears (published by Regal Books).

Study Bibles—Many excellent study Bibles are available to help the student. These may include commentaries and concordances and insightful articles or footnotes. The study Bible recommended for use with this course is *The NIV Student Bible* published by Zondervan Bible Publishers. The goal of the editors of *The NIV Student Bible* was to produce a version that ordinary people could and would read on a regular, sustained basis without getting discouraged. They accomplished this goal admirably.

METHODS

Here are a few things you can do to help make your Bible study time more meaningful:

Develop a method of marking your Bible. This can be as simple as underlining passages or words that have particular significance for you, or it can be more elaborate. Some Bible students use various colors of pens or pencils to highlight different things (red for prophetic passages, blue for discipleship themes, etc.).

Keep notes. Write down questions, insights and personal applications. Research your questions.

Paraphrase. Writing a passage in your own words will increase your understanding of it.

The optional session "The Process of Bible Study" presents this material to the members of your group. If you will not be teaching this session, you may want to photocopy the student handout and distribute it to the class as a resource.

LYRICS FOR THE LIVING GOD

The psalms were meant to be sung—and shouted

Sing to him a new song; play skillfully, and shout for joy. Psalm 33:3

William Booth, believing the nineteenth-century English church had become too refined to reach the cities' poor, took the gospel into the streets. He organized his workers into a "salvation army," complete with uniforms and military rank.

With hecklers and drunks abounding, the "army" didn't always find preaching easy or safe. A local builder, Charles William Fry, offered himself and his three sons as bodyguards. As it happened, all four played brass instruments, which they carried along to accompany their singing.

Booth's rowdier supporters were soon dragging along concertinas, bells, hunting horns, banjos, tambourines, and drums to praise the Lord. Said one leader, "It sounds as if a brass band's gone out of its mind."

Salvation Army recruits did not stick to traditional hymns but invented their own words for rousing popular tunes. "Here's to Good Old Whiskey" became "Storm the Forts of Darkness." Booth had his doubts about this trend until one night, hearing a beautiful rendition of "Bless His Name, He Sets Me Free," he asked about the tune. "Why, Mr. Booth, that's 'Champagne Charlie Is My Name,'" the embarrassed singer replied.

"That settles it," Booth said. "Why *should* the devil have all the best tunes?" Soon 400 bands were crashing about England, playing hit tunes with Christian words.

The Best Music Available

David and his people would have liked that spirit. Many of the psalms were meant to be sung, and sung joyfully. Modern church formality seems far removed from their frequent command: "Sing for joy! Shout aloud!" Their instruments included cymbals, tambourines, trumpets, ram's horns, harps, and lyres. Sometimes dancing erupted. The world, in the psalmist's imagination, can't contain the delight God inspires. A *new* song must be sung. "Shout for joy to the Lord, all the earth, burst into jubilant song" (Psalm 98:4).

First Chronicles 15:16 and 23:5 report that David appointed 4,000 professional musicians to provide their services to the temple. They offered the best music available, and the congregation joined in. Nobody knows exactly what it sounded like, but scholars doubt it was all soft and soothing. Musicians improvised. Most of the instruments used suggest rousing, rhythmic sound.

Every generation of Christians renews the discovery of this "new song," sometimes through the music of their forebears, sometimes in a form that shocks their solemn elders. The Salvation Army did, and so did the Jesus Movement of the sixties. David would not have been surprised. He jolted his own wife with spontaneous dancing (see 1 Chronicles 15:29). When people know God, they come to life with a jubilant song on their lips.

Reprinted from *The NIV Student Bible* with permission from Zondervan Bible Publishers.

THE PLEDGE*

It's a world of choices patterned to confuse.
Distracting little voices whisper what to do.
Searching for the pieces one step from the edge.
Turn your heart toward Jesus.
Make this solemn pledge,

He died for me. I'll live for Him.
He died for me. I'll live for Him.

Above all lords and regents,
He is the King of kings.
I'm pledging my allegiance
through these words I sing.
Take this oath of service.
Write it on your wall.
It's our only purpose
for living life at all.

He died for me. I'll live for Him.
He died for me. I'll live for Him.

STEP 1 — TAKE THE PLEDGE

Theme: Discipleship begins with a decision to follow Jesus.

Memory Verse: *Repent, then, and turn to God, so that your sins may be wiped out, that times of refreshing may come from the Lord.* Acts 3:19

Checklist

You and your students will know that you have accomplished the goals of this Bible study session if:
- ❏ You understand the problem of sin.
- ❏ You have repented and turned from sin.
- ❏ You have placed your faith in Jesus.
- ❏ You have surrendered to Jesus as Lord.
- ❏ You have publicly confessed your faith in Jesus and your decision to follow Him.

Materials
- Bibles;
- Paper and pencils or pens;
- A photocopy of the lyrics of "The Pledge" and of the Self-Evaluation Sheet for each student. (If you wish, you may copy the self evaluation onto the reverse side of the lyrics to save paper.);

Options
- The album or the video *The Pledge* by DeGarmo and Key (available at most Christian bookstores).

*From the 1989 album *The Pledge* by D&K; all other lyrics in this course are from *Go to the Top*, D&K's 1991 release.
© 1991 DKB Music/ASCAP. All rights reserved. Used by permission. Permission to photocopy granted.

THE PLEDGE

It's a world of choices patterned to confuse.
Distracting little voices whisper what to do.
Searching for the pieces one step from the edge.
Turn your heart toward Jesus.
Make this solemn pledge.

He died for me. I'll live for Him.
He died for me. I'll live for Him.

Above all lords and regents
He is the King of kings.
I'm pledging my allegiance
through these words I sing.
Take this oath of service.
Write it on your wall.
It's our only purpose
for living life at all.

He died for me. I'll live for Him.
He died for me. I'll live for Him.

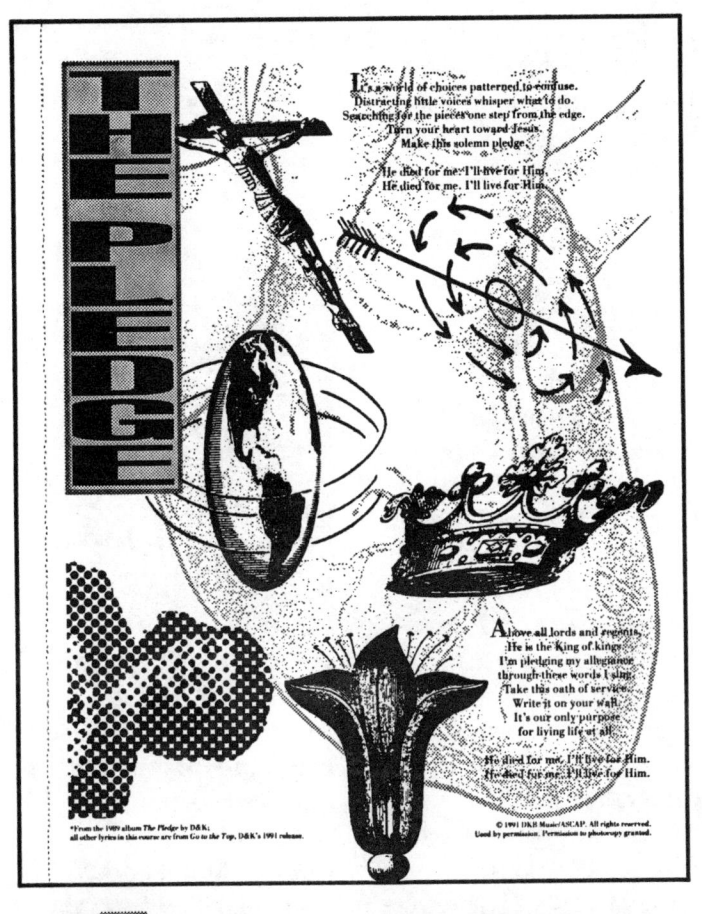

*From the 1989 album The Pledge by D&K; all other lyrics in this course are from Go to the Top, D&K's 1991 release.
© 1991 D&K Music/ASCAP. All rights reserved. Used by permission. Permission to photocopy granted.

1 BEGIN

Hand out the lyrics to "The Pledge." If you have *The Pledge* album or video, play the title cut as your students follow along with the lyrics.

Ask, **Why do you think DeGarmo and Key used the images they did for this song?** Encourage discussion by reacting positively to the suggestions offered by the students.

Read the first line of the song aloud and say, **What choices do you think DeGarmo and Key are talking about?** Allow two or three minutes for answers. Then say something like this, **Let's pretend for a moment that I'm a stranger here. I heard somebody say something about God and I started asking questions. What would you say if I said, "Okay, so maybe God is real. So what? What does God have to do with me?"**

Field their answers. As soon as someone mentions God, say, still playing the part of the stranger, **Who is God, anyway?** Write on a chalkboard or overhead projector, "Who is God?" As soon as someone mentions Jesus, say, **Who is Jesus?** Write down this question. (Leave space between the questions as you write them down.) Keep discussing the question "Who is Jesus?" until someone mentions Jesus dying for us. Say and write, **Why did Jesus die for us?**

2 WHO IS GOD?

Next say something like, **We're going to get back to basics for a few minutes and address these three questions. For this first question, I want you to get into groups of three or four people.** Have them get into their groups and quieted down before you continue with instructions.

Hand out a blank piece of paper and pencil to each group. Say, **You've probably all heard the children's story of Pinocchio, but in case you haven't let me tell you a little about it.** Briefly tell about Gepetto, the toymaker, who was lonely and made a little wooden boy to keep him company. Be sure to mention that Pinocchio was a very naughty wooden boy who kept getting into trouble but was finally able to become a real boy because he deserved it. Say, **There are some parallels between this story and the story of the human condition. I want you to write down what you think are the parallels and the differences.**

Optional: Instead of simply writing and discussing their ideas, students may retell the story as it would be told if Gepetto was God and Pinocchio represented humankind. Let them use any medium of story telling they would like. For instance, they could use a skit, ballad, rap, or narration.

As students perform or tell what they wrote down, make short notes on the chalkboard or overhead as answers to the three questions are revealed. For instance, that Gepetto created Pinocchio and God created humans will most likely be brought out. A major difference you will want to mention is that in the children's story, Pinocchio earns his rebirth as a real boy. In no way, however, can

11

Christians earn their spiritual rebirth in Christ. It is a part of salvation which is God's gift (see Eph. 2:8,9).

Very quickly go over the answers to "Who is God?" that come as a result of the preceding exercise. Add any essential information that was not discussed by the students.

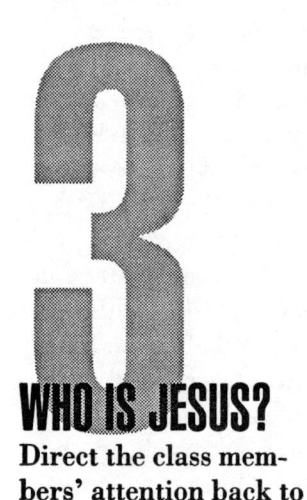

3 WHO IS JESUS?

Direct the class members' attention back to the lyric sheets. Say, **What words in this song might help us answer the question, "Who is Jesus?"** Write down the students' responses next to the question, "Who is Jesus?"

Next say, **Let's take a look at some of the things Jesus said about Himself.** Have volunteers read the following verses: John 8:12; John 10:11; John 11:25; and John 14:6. Write one of the following headings on four separate pieces of newsprint—a different heading on each—as students read the corresponding verses: The Light of the World; The Good Shepherd; The Resurrection and the Life; The Way, the Truth and the Life.

Encourage the students to brainstorm about what Jesus might be telling about Himself through these analogies. Write the ideas down on the newsprint with the matching headline.

Ask your students to look again at John 14:6. Begin reading that verse aloud and continue reading through verse 11. Say something like, **This is something Jesus says about Himself in relation to God the Father. In John 10:30 Jesus says, "I and the Father are one."** Under the question "Who is Jesus?" write "God." Then say, **In John 14:16 Jesus begins speaking of the Holy Spirit, the third Person of the Godhead. We'll talk more about the Holy Spirit in another lesson.**

4 WHY DID JESUS DIE FOR US?

Direct your students' attention to the third question, "Why did Jesus die for us?" Have your students turn to Genesis 3. Ask for a volunteer who knows the story of Adam and Eve being expelled from the garden. Have the volunteer tell the story. Gently correct any errors in the telling. (Make sure you have a thorough grasp of the story yourself.) Read aloud Genesis 3:15 explaining that this verse anticipated the birth of Jesus.

Have your students turn to Romans 3:10-12. After a volunteer reads the verses, ask, **What is the relationship between these verses and the story of Adam and Eve?** The answer you are looking for is that because of the fall of humankind, we are all sinners.

Move down to verse 20 in Romans 3. Have a volunteer read the verse and put it in his or her own words.

Read aloud verse 21 through verse 26. Say, **This answers the question "Why did Jesus die for us?" Can anybody tell me, based on the last few verses we've looked at, why Jesus died for us?** The answer should include the following parts: we are sinners; our relationship with God has been broken; we can't earn it back by being "good"; Jesus died as a sacrifice to restore our relationship with God.

Optional: Should someone ask, "But why was a sacrifice necessary?", read together the Insight on page 111 of *The NIV Student Bible*. This article discusses God's justice and His requirement that sin must be atoned before we can fellowship with Him. If you do not have *The NIV Student Bible*, refer to these verses: Leviticus 4:27-35; Hebrews 10:1-10.

Say something like, **A lot of us, like Pinocchio, think that if we just try harder to be good, we can become real and earn our way to heaven. But there is simply no way we can ever be that good. When we are finally allowed to be with God, it will be because God made it possible by giving us the gift of His Son. That gift given when we are so undeserving is called "grace."**

5 ACCEPTING THE GIFT

Have a volunteer read Romans 6:23. Ask, **How do we accept that gift?** Write down their answers on a chalkboard or overhead projector. Have everyone turn to Acts 2:37-39 and Romans 10:9 to see if they've listed everything. Make sure the following are included: confess that Jesus is Lord; accept Jesus as Lord; believe God raised Him from the dead; repent and be baptized; ask for forgiveness.

Say, **After you accept Jesus, what happens? Here's something that Dana Key has to say:**

Optional: Set up the video, *The Pledge*, to begin at the following statement. (On the tape this comes in the interview section before the song "The Pledge.")

Read aloud the following statement if you don't use the video:

It would be wonderful if we could just say, "Jesus, come into my life, forgive me of my sins," and then all of a sudden we die and He zaps us into heaven. And really, that would be a lot easier. I spoke to a youth group the other night and I said, "If Jesus were here and He asked you to give your life, how many of you would?" Everybody raised their hand. Because, in that one moment of time we might be able to work up enough spirituality to say, "Yeah, Jesus, You died for me and I'll die for You." But Jesus asks us to do something that is really more difficult than that. He asks us to live for Him and that is a very difficult thing to do.

Ask your students, **What makes it so difficult to live for**

13

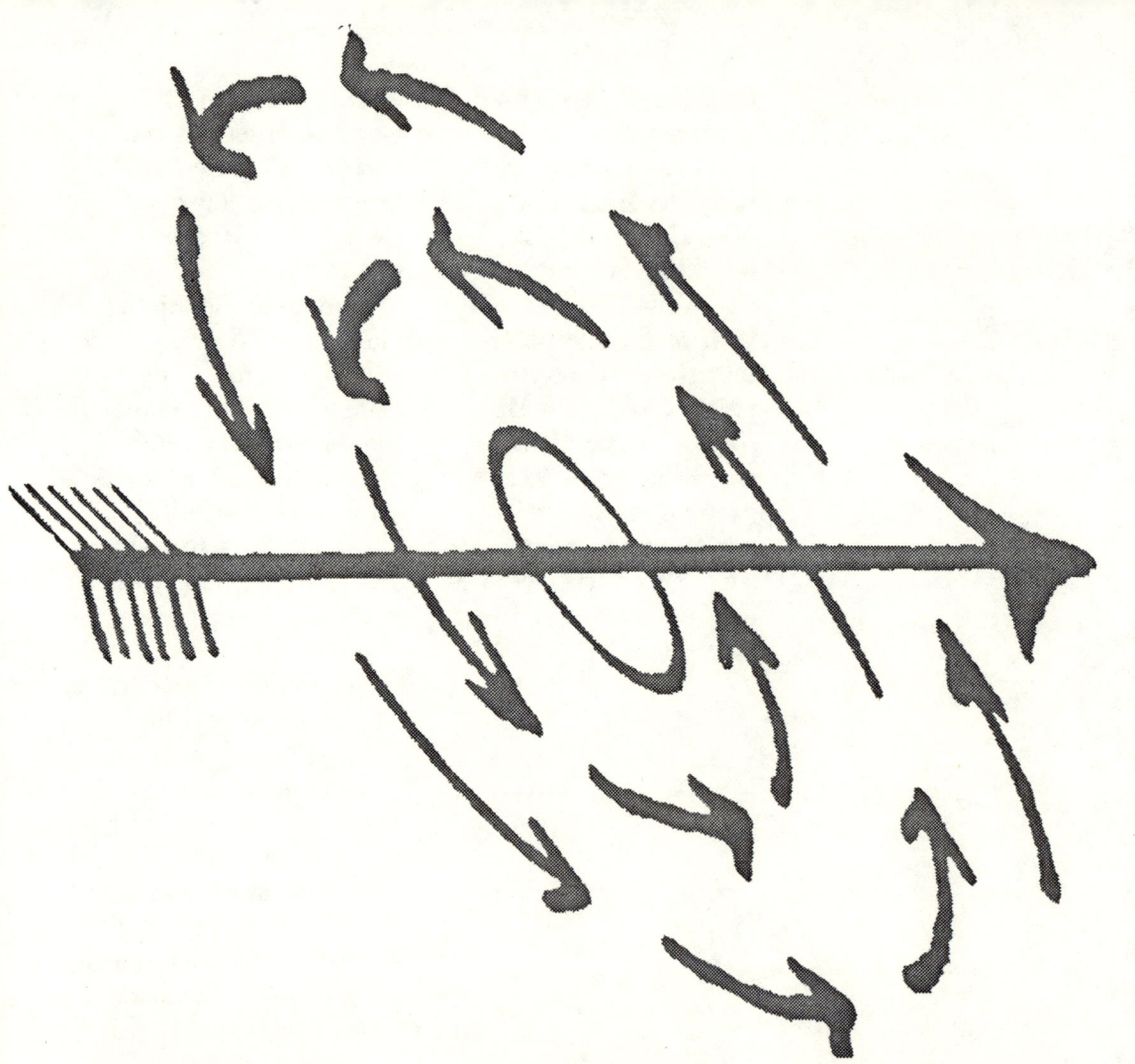

Jesus? Listen to their answers. Wait for an answer that deals with the fact that we'd rather live for ourselves. If no one comes up with that answer in a few minutes, say it yourself. If someone does, repeat it or rephrase it in these words: **It's hard for us to live for Jesus because we'd rather live for ourselves.** Then say, **In the beginning of this time together we talked about the "world of choices" that DeGarmo and Key sang about. I want to suggest that our ultimate choice is: Who are we going to live for—Jesus or ourselves?**

Say, **Bob Dylan wrote a song that talks about how no matter who you are, you have to serve somebody. Whether you serve the devil or the Lord is up to you. But, we all serve somebody.**

Optional: Play Bob Dylan's "Gotta Serve Somebody" from the album *Slow Train Coming*. After one chorus, turn it down low and say the following:

In the Satanic Bible, there is a list of commandments—a kind of takeoff on our Holy Bible's Ten Commandments. Our first two commandments are about worshiping God, no one or nothing else. In the Satanic Bible, the first commandment is not about worshiping Satan, as you might think. It's about serving yourself. This is something to think about. Satan is happy when we serve ourselves. He knows this means we're not serving Jesus.

Distribute the Self-Evaluation Sheet for students to work on at home.

Close in prayer.

OPTIONAL LOCK-IN:

To kick off this course, you may want to do this first session at a lock-in or other type of overnighter. Activities to include at the lock-in might be:

- Show the entire video of *The Pledge*;
- Prepare in advance to have a baptismal service for those who are ready to make this public confession of faith. Invite the congregation to attend this part of the overnighter.
- Have students make a poster (or posters) using the second verse and chorus from the lyrics of "The Pledge."
- Ask class members to write up a class covenant declaring their desire to serve Jesus and make Him Lord of their lives. Only those who are certain of their desire to follow through with this pledge should sign the covenant.

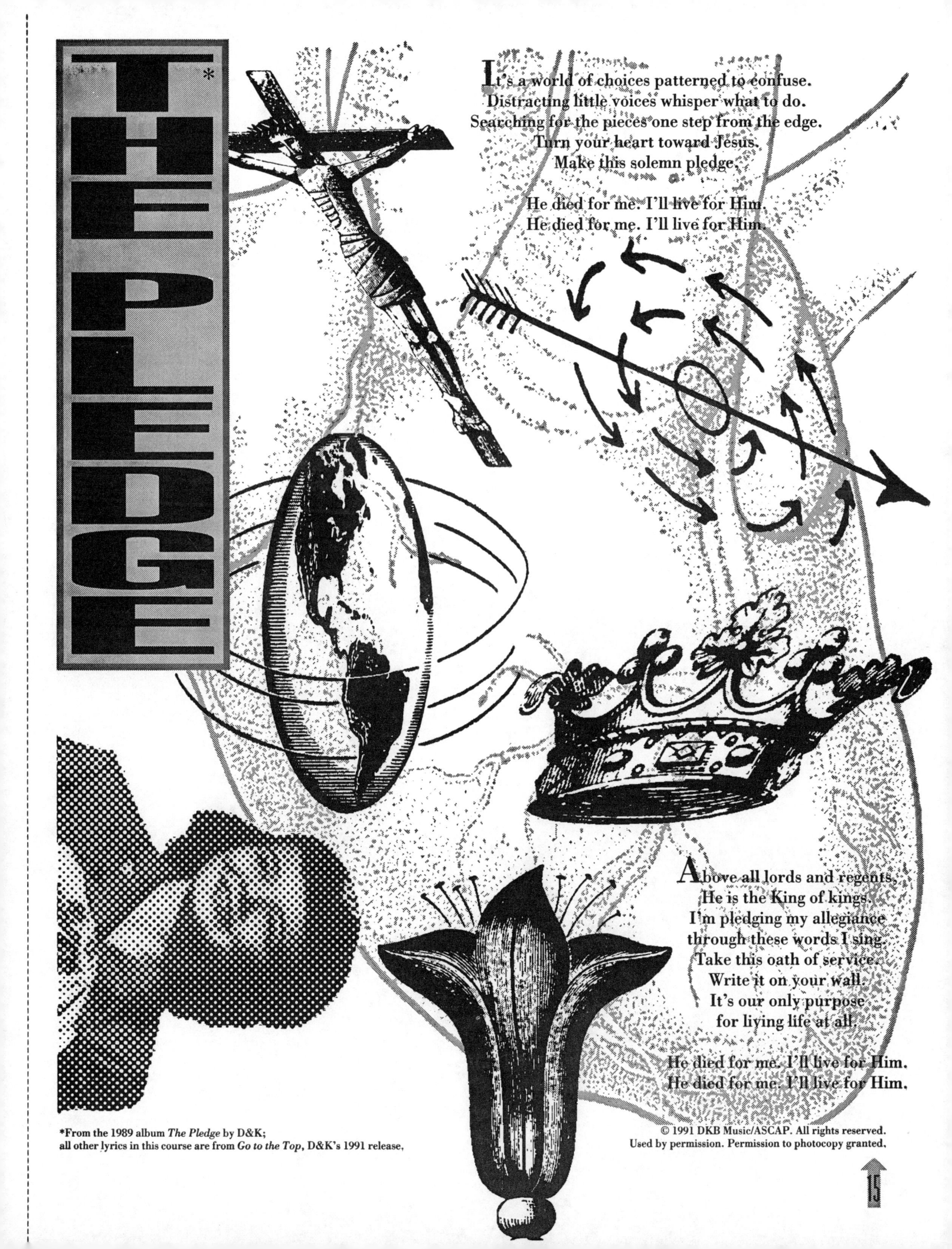

THE PLEDGE*

It's a world of choices patterned to confuse.
Distracting little voices whisper what to do.
Searching for the pieces one step from the edge.
Turn your heart toward Jesus.
Make this solemn pledge.

He died for me. I'll live for Him.
He died for me. I'll live for Him.

Above all lords and regents,
He is the King of kings.
I'm pledging my allegiance
through these words I sing.
Take this oath of service.
Write it on your wall.
It's our only purpose
for living life at all.

He died for me. I'll live for Him.
He died for me. I'll live for Him.

*From the 1989 album *The Pledge* by D&K;
all other lyrics in this course are from *Go to the Top*, D&K's 1991 release.

© 1991 DKB Music/ASCAP. All rights reserved.
Used by permission. Permission to photocopy granted.

STEP 1 TAKE THE PLEDGE
THE PLEDGE
SELF-EVALUATION SHEET

Memory Verse: *Repent, then, and turn to God, so that your sins may be wiped out, that times of refreshing may come from the Lord.* Acts 3:19

Personal Evaluation: Respond honestly to the statements below. Then score your responses. Use this evaluation to help you as you complete the Personal Journal section.

	Almost Always	Usually	Rarely
Having repented and turned to Jesus, I vigilantly resist sin.	❏	❏	❏
My daily strength and hope comes from my faith in Jesus.	❏	❏	❏
I submit my actions each day to the Lord; I strive to honor Him.	❏	❏	❏
I publicly confess my faith in Jesus.	❏	❏	❏

Scoring
Give yourself three points for every "almost always" answer, one point for every "usually" and zero points for "rarely."

- **9-12** You are a committed disciple.
- **6-8** You are well on your way to becoming a mature, committed disciple.
- **0-5** You need to reexamine your commitment and take steps to follow through.

Personal Journal
What characteristic about the Lord and His concern for you particularly affected you during the class session?

Just as married couples' love can grow and take on new dimensions of commitment, so can your relationship with the Lord grow (even if you are already a committed disciple). What can you do to improve your commitment to Christ this week?

Read again the Bible Memory Verse (see top of page). Commit it to your memory. What do you think is meant by "times of refreshing"? What times of refreshing has the Lord given you?

© 1991 DeGarmo and Key by Gospel Light. All rights reserved. Permission to photocopy granted.

BIBLEIEVE

> Don't need no money,
> don't need no title,
> don't trust in things that you can see or feel.
> I trust my Savior,
> I trust my Bible,
> I trust in God because I know He's real.
>
> Whoa, I believe in Jesus;
> whoa, I believe His Word.
> Whoa, I believe in Jesus;
> whoa, I believe in His Word.
>
> Don't love the new age,
> don't love the devil,
> don't love a world where people lie and steal.
> I trust my Savior,
> and I trust my Bible;
> I trust in God because I know He's real.
>
> Whoa, I believe in Jesus;
> whoa, I believe His Word.
> Whoa, I believe in Jesus;
> whoa, I believe in His Word.

STEP 2 READ THE WORD

Theme: "Feeding" on God's Word produces spiritual victory, growth and blessings.

Memory Verse: *Like newborn babies, crave pure spiritual milk, so that by it you may grow up in your salvation, now that you have tasted that the Lord is good.* 1 Peter 2:2,3

Checklist

You and your students will know that you have accomplished the goals of this Bible study session if:

- ❑ You believe the Bible is God's Word.
- ❑ You have a basic understanding of the Bible's contents and purpose.
- ❑ You read and study the Word.
- ❑ You hear the Bible taught.

Materials

- Bibles;
- Paper and pencils or pens;
- A photocopy of the lyrics of "I Believe" and of the Step 2 Self-Evaluation Sheet for each class member;

Optional

- The album *Go to the Top* by DeGarmo and Key (available at most Christian bookstores);
- For object lessons: a stack of love letters (real or simulated) tied with a ribbon; a compass; a mirror; a how-to manual; a guidebook; a watering can; some nourishing food; a facsimile of a sword;

© 1991 DKB Music/ASCAP. All rights reserved. Used by permission. Permission to photocopy granted.

- "love letters" from God—envelopes containing letters with the following Scriptures written out (one per envelope): John 3:16; John 15:9; 1 John 3:1a; 1 John 3:16a; 1 John 4:9; 1 John 4:10. Sign the letters, "I love you. God";
- six copies of the skit "Pass the A-1 Sauce" and the props listed on the skit sheet. You will need six people, two males and four females, to perform the skit. If you want a more polished performance, have volunteers practice the skit at some point before class.

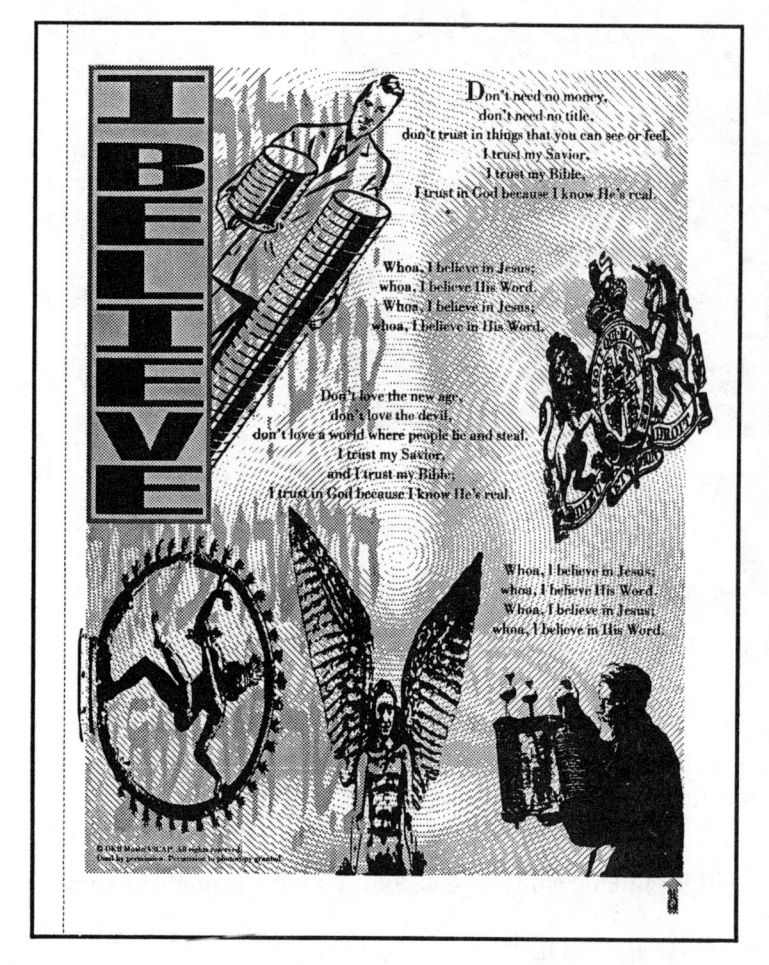

I BELIEVE

Don't need no money,
don't need no title,
don't trust in things that you can see or feel.
I trust my Savior,
I trust my Bible.
I trust in God because I know He's real.

Whoa, I believe in Jesus;
whoa, I believe His Word.
Whoa, I believe in Jesus;
whoa, I believe in His Word.

Don't love the new age,
don't love the devil,
don't love a world where people lie and steal.
I trust my Savior,
and I trust my Bible;
I trust in God because I know He's real.

Whoa, I believe in Jesus;
whoa, I believe His Word.
Whoa, I believe in Jesus;
whoa, I believe in His Word.

SKIT
PASS THE A-1 SAUCE

Characters
Huey: An immature Christian teenager
Josh: Huey's friend
Sara, Lee, Lorna and Doon: Huey's wish list of girlfriends

Props: Lunch sacks, lunch food, a teen-sized diaper, a baby bottle, a tape of *Age to Age* by Amy Grant, cued up to "Fat Baby," a tape player. Optional—Baby bonnet, rattle, rubber duckie.

Sara, Lee, Lorna and Doon are brown-bagging it in their school lunch area. Huey enters wearing nothing but a large diaper over a pair of shorts. He has a bottle in one hand. Other costume accessories for Huey might be: a baby bonnet, a rattle, a rubber duckie. Lorna sees Huey.

Lorna: (calling to Huey): Hi, cutie-pie. Where've you been? Want to eat lunch with us?
Huey: (Trying to be cool): I don't know. Some of the cheerleaders wanted me to eat with them. (He pauses.) What the heck, I might as well give you girls the pleasure of my company.
Sara: (faking sweetness): How condescending of you.
Huey: (modestly): I try my best. Hey, what are you guys doing Saturday night? I'm gonna have a party at my house. No parents, but plenty of other stuff. (He waves his bottle.) Want to come?

The girls look uncomfortable.

Lee: Sorry. I'm baby-sitting.
Lorna: I've gotta study.
Doon: I'm going out with Josh. Somewhere else.
Huey: You mean Josh won't come, either? (He turns to Sara.) How about you, Sexy?
Sara: (choking): I have to wash my cat.
Huey: (takes a long pull on his bottle; to Sara): You don't like me, do you?
Lee: Huey, don't—
Sara: I like you fine. It's just...the way you act sometimes.
Doon: (trying to break the tension): Hey, there's Josh.
Huey: (eager to get away): Oh, I need to talk to him. See you guys later.

Josh enters as Huey runs over to him.

Huey: Josh, you've gotta help me. I'm dying over there.
Josh: What's the matter, Bud?
Huey: Okay, here's the thing. I know some of those girls like me—they tickle me under the chin and play "This Little Piggy" with me and all. But whenever I ask them to go anywhere, none of them want to go. You're in with Doon. Do they ever talk about me? What's the deal?
Josh: Well, I did hear them talking once. About you. I'm not sure you want to hear it.
Huey: (getting down on his knees and clasping his hands together): Oh, I do I do I do. Tell me.
Josh: Okay. They were like, um, rating the guys in the school.
Huey: They do that, too?
Josh: Not exactly the same, but kinda. And Lee brought up you...and they agreed you were kind of cute, but....
Huey: What! But what!
Josh: Well, it was like this....

Music to "Fat Baby," from Amy Grant's Age to Age begins playing. The girls get up from their lunch and lip-sync the song. SARA takes the lead, the others sing back-up. Choreograph it with motions like the Lennon Sisters may have used in the fifties or with soft-shoe dancing. When the girls finish singing, they sit down and resume eating.

Huey: Oh, this is worse than I thought. They think I'm like a baby?
Josh: Well, you know you've been a Christian for as long as the rest of us, but for some reason, you're still wearing diapers.
Huey: I am? (He looks down at his diaper.) Oh my gosh! I am! What am I gonna do?
Josh: Well, for starters, you could start coming to Bible study.
Huey: (whining): But that's at the same time as my favorite TV program.
Josh: (sarcastically): That *is* a dilemma.
Huey: Yeah.

Huey looks over at the girls and suddenly remembers he's wearing a diaper. He begins to pull at it.

Oh my gosh. This diaper! Do you think the girls noticed?
Josh: What are you doing? You can't just take it off. (He propels HUEY towards the exit.) Go get some decent clothes, first.
Huey: Yeah, I guess you're right. Hmmmmm, maybe I should rethink this Bible study stuff. Will the girls be there?
Josh: Yeah, they'll be there. But you're gonna get more out of it than just seeing them.
Huey: Like what?

Josh takes Huey's bottle and tosses it up in the air as they walk toward the exit.

Josh: Ever had steak?
Huey shakes his head.

© DeGarmo and Key by Gospel Light. All rights reserved. Permission to photocopy granted.

---

1 BEGIN

Hand out a copy of the lyrics to "I Believe" (from the album *Go to the Top*) to each student. Read the lyrics together, or play the song while all follow along, reading the lyrics.

Optional: While you play the song "I Believe," let students experience a Trust Fall: Have them get in groups of six—five people form a closed circle, one crosses his arms in front of his chest and stands in the middle. The student in the center closes his eyes and, keeping his body stiff, allows himself to fall forward, backward, sideways. The students who form the circle gently push the inside student to help him back to an upward stance. During the song, each student in the circle should be allowed a turn in the center. After the song is finished, ask the students how they felt about being in the center.

Ask, **Did you ever feel completely sure you would not fall?** Allow a minute or two for responses. Then say something like, **Even though we might trust people, there's almost always a little skepticism, because we know that no one, or no thing, can be entirely trustworthy. The exception is God and His Word.**

If you do not use the Trust Fall, ask these questions:
- Is there anyone you trust unconditionally?
- Have you ever trusted someone and been let down?
- Do you think God and the Bible can be trusted?
- Why or why not?

2

WHAT IS THE BIBLE?

Note—For better visual impact, have the objects used in the following object lessons displayed at the front of (or around) the room. Objects: a stack of love letters (simulated or real) tied with ribbon; a compass; a mirror; a how-to manual; a guidebook; a watering can; some nourishing food; a facsimile of a sword. You may want to handle the objects as you come to each in the lesson. If you don't have the actual objects, write these words on newsprint or a chalkboard: love letters; compass; mirror; how-to manual; guidebook; stream; food; sword. Mix up the order and post the words where all can easily see them.

Say, **Today we're going to talk about the Bible. I'm going to use several objects to demonstrate what the Bible is to Christians.**

Next say something like, **Let's begin with these love letters. How do they relate to the Bible?** Allow time for thoughtful answers. If the following analogies are not brought up, you may want to suggest them yourself: God speaks to us using the written word; the Bible is full of words of love from God to us; getting love letters from the person we love should make us eager to read what is inside.

Optional: Ask, **Have any of you ever thought of writing a love letter back to God?** Hand a love letter from the stack to each student. The love letters should have one of the following, or similar, Scriptures written out: John 3:16; John 15:9; 1 John 3:1a; 1 John 3:16a; 1 John 4:9; 1 John 4:10. Sign the love letters, "I love you. God." Hand out paper and envelopes for your students to write love letters back to God.

Ask your students to turn to 2 Timothy 3:16,17. Ask a volunteer to read this passage. Then ask, **What do you think the statement, "All Scripture is God-breathed" means?** Allow time for responses The following points should be brought out: another word for "God-breathed" is "inspired"; the Bible is not just words and letters—God was the source of this production.

Drawing attention to either the objects you brought in for the object lessons or the words you have written and posted, say, **Four of these objects fit this passage in some way or another. Anyone want to take a guess at which ones they are?** The correct objects are the compass, the mirror, the how-to manual and the guidebook. In response to wrong answers, say, **Well, that might fit, but that's not the object I'm thinking of.** When you hear a correct answer, circle the word or hold up the object. When all four have been guessed, continue with the lesson.

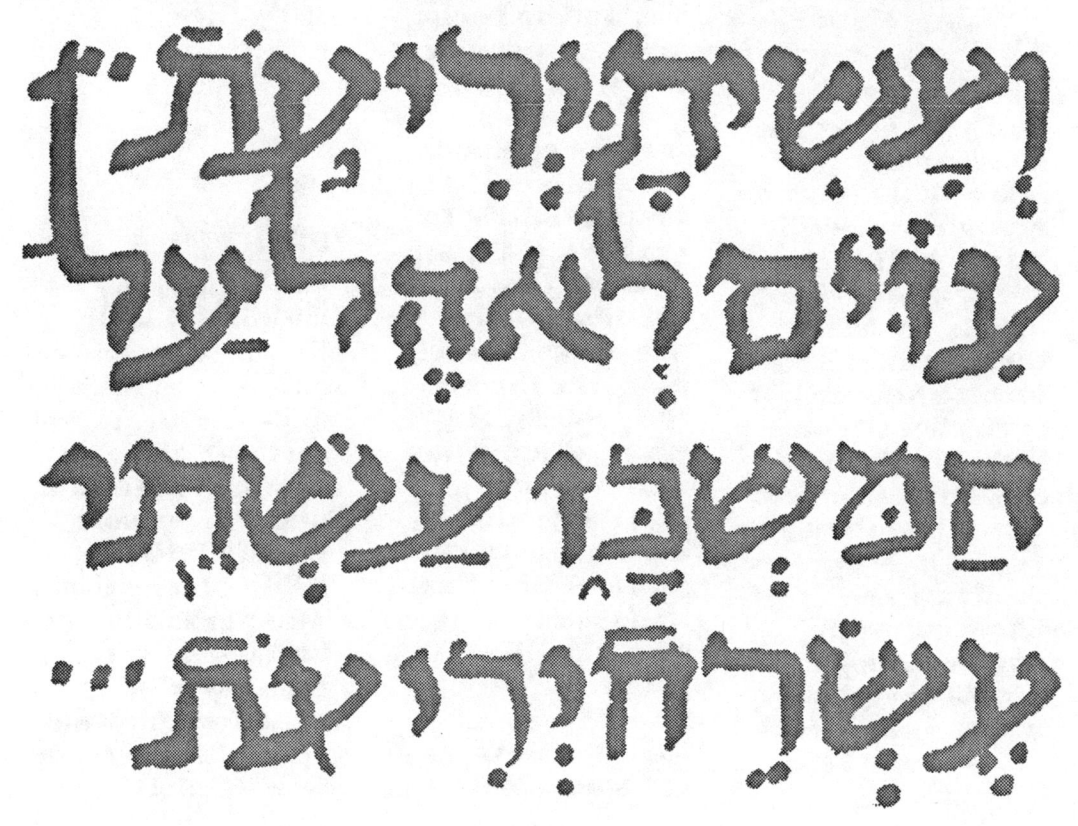

Say something like, **I want to use the compass as an example of "training in righteousness." Does anybody see the connection and want to share it with us?** The point you want to bring out is that a compass, like Scripture, shows us the way to go, shows us when we're getting off track. If we use the Bible a lot and know it well, it will be pretty clear to us when we are doing something we are not supposed to do, or not doing something we should.

Ask a volunteer to read James 1:22-25. Say, **James refers to the Bible as a mirror; something to look into to check how we're doing. Can you think of an art where mirrors are used a lot?** The answer you are looking for is ballet or other individual dancing. You may need to help the class by giving them a hint. If so, say something like, **If you've ever seen a dance studio, you know that the walls are covered with mirrors. This is so the dancers will be able to perfect their form. It's hard to know what each part of your body is doing at any given moment. You might think you're doing pretty good in your Christian walk until you look into the Bible and see where your form is off. In a way, the Bible helps us to correct our posture.**

Optional: Ask for a volunteer (one who is wearing pants). Have the volunteer get down on her elbows and knees with her arms resting on the ground in front. Tell her you want her elbows directly under her shoulders and one leg lifted back so that it is directly parallel to the floor. She should then bend the knee of that leg so that it is exactly perpendicular to the floor. Have another volunteer then hold up a large mirror so that the student can perfect the stance. Other students may want to try as well, to find out how difficult it is to know exactly what one's own body is doing without a reflection. Have a discussion on what the students learned.

Refer to the how-to manual. Say something like, **How-to books are very popular. If I want to know how to take pictures of animals, there are books out there that will tell me how. If I want to know how to rebuild a VW, there are books that will guide me through the process. If I want to know how to live a Christian life, there are books. And the first and foremost how-to book for living a Christian life is the Bible.**

Refer to the guidebook. Ask, **How is a guidebook different from a how-to book?** Write down the responses on the chalkboard, newsprint or overhead transparency. Help the responses along by saying, **Suppose I had a book called <u>Africa on $5 a Day</u>. What might that book tell me?** Possible answers: where to stay, things to see, what food to avoid, places not to miss. Say, **All right, now compare this to the Bible.** Write these responses down, too. Be sure to include that the Bible guides us toward a better and more enjoyable stay on earth.

3
SPIRITUAL NOURISHMENT

Have the class members turn to Psalm 1:2,3. Ask a volunteer to read the verses. Say, **The psalmist is talking about a person who is into the Bible all the time. The person is symbolized by a tree. What symbol is used for spiritual refreshment from God's Spirit?** The

22

answer you are looking for is "streams of water" (Ps. 63:1; Isa. 44:3; Jer. 2:13; John 7:37-39).

Optional: Lead the class through an exercise in making up a verse that is about a person who never studies the Bible, using the same type of symbolism. An example would be: "But his delight is not in the law of the Lord, and on MTV he meditates day and night. He is like a tree planted in the desert, which never produces any fruit and whose leaf is always withered. Whatever he does comes to nothing."

Ask, **What does Psalm 1:2,3 say that studying the Bible and thinking about it will do for a person?** Allow a minute or to for responses.

Direct the class to turn to 1 Peter 2:2,3 and ask a volunteer to read these verses aloud. Ask, **What happens to a baby who doesn't receive food?** After responses, say, **In a few places the Bible refers to the things Scripture teaches us as something to be eaten. What do you think happens to new Christians who don't eat their spiritual food—who don't study the Bible?**

Optional: This is the time to put on the skit "Pass the A-1 Sauce" if you will be using it. Hand out copies of the skit and props to volunteers (if you did not prepare the performance before class). You will need two male and four female performers. Let the volunteers look over the skit while you have the rest of the class turn to Hebrews 5:11-14. Ask a volunteer to read the passage. Say something like, **The writer of Hebrews takes the analogy of Scripture being milk a step further. The writer is saying that the basics of Scripture are like milk to a baby, but as you grow older, you need more of the meat of Scripture—you can't mature on just milk.** Announce that the skit players will now present, "Pass the A-1 Sauce."

4
THE ARMOR OF GOD

Ask the class if anyone knows where the famous passage about the armor of God is located in the Bible. Have everyone turn to that passage, beginning with Ephesians 6:13. Ask a volunteer to read through verse 17. Say, **As this passage is read, think about the kind of armor that is being talked about.** After the passage is read, ask,

5. WHO SAYS THE BIBLE HAS AUTHORITY AND POWER?

Say, **There's a famous encounter between Jesus and the devil when Jesus quoted Scripture to defeat Satan. Does anyone know what that encounter is sometimes called, or can anyone find it in their Bible?** The answer you are looking for is that it's sometimes called "The Temptation of Christ" and it can be found mentioned in Mark and detailed in Matthew and Luke. If there is time, have your students turn to Matthew 4:1-11. You might want to point out that the devil also used Scripture to try to tempt Christ, so it is important that we know Scripture well enough to know when it is being used in the wrong way.

Say something like, **Even though Jesus, being the Son of God, had authority on His own, He used the authority of Scripture against the devil. That presents a good case for the authenticity and power of the Bible. In other words, going back to the song by DeGarmo and Key, you can trust the Bible to be God's Word.**

Ask half of the class to turn to Joshua 1:8 and the other half to Psalm 119:11. Then say something like, **When we were studying the verse about the streams of water, we learned that a fulfilled person meditates on Scripture and is spiritually refreshed. The Bible suggests that meditating on Scripture means to think about it and apply it to one's own life. So I'd like you to meditate on your choice of the verses we've used in this session.**

If you did not copy the Self-Evaluation Sheet onto the reverse side of the "I Believe" lyrics, hand them out at this time. Class members are to work on these personal applications at home. Suggest that students who own *The NIV Student Bible* look at pages 16 through 18 sometime during the week for a good overview of the Old and New Testaments.

Close in prayer.

Which of these pieces of armor is the Word of God? (The sword.) After a correct response, say, **Can anyone tell me what the main difference is between this piece of armor and the other pieces of armor?** The answer you are looking for is that the sword, or the Bible, is one of the only three offensive weapons that is mentioned. The shoes of sharing the gospel (Eph. 6:15) and prayer by the Spirit's guidance (Eph. 6:18) are the other weapons. The other pieces of armor are all defensive.

Go back to Ephesians 6:11 and read that verse. Say something like, **We put on the defensive armor (truth, righteousness, peace, faith, salvation) so that when the devil tries to get at us, we are protected against him. The weapon we have to put him back in his place is Scripture.**

I BELIEVE

Don't need no money,
don't need no title,
don't trust in things that you can see or feel.
I trust my Savior,
I trust my Bible,
I trust in God because I know He's real.

Whoa, I believe in Jesus;
whoa, I believe His Word.
Whoa, I believe in Jesus;
whoa, I believe in His Word.

Don't love the new age,
don't love the devil,
don't love a world where people lie and steal.
I trust my Savior,
and I trust my Bible;
I trust in God because I know He's real.

Whoa, I believe in Jesus;
whoa, I believe His Word.
Whoa, I believe in Jesus;
whoa, I believe in His Word.

© 1991 DKB Music/ASCAP. All rights reserved.
Used by permission. Permission to photocopy granted.

SKIT
PASS THE A-1 SAUCE

Characters
Huey: An immature Christian teenager
Josh: Huey's friend
Sara, Lee, Lorna and Doon: Huey's wish list of girlfriends

Props: Lunch sacks, lunch food, a teen-sized diaper, a baby bottle, a tape of *Age to Age* by Amy Grant, cued up to "Fat Baby," a tape player. Optional—Baby bonnet, rattle, rubber duckie.

Sara, Lee, Lorna and Doon are brown-bagging it in their school lunch area. Huey enters wearing nothing but a large diaper over a pair of shorts. He has a bottle in one hand. Other costume accessories for Huey might be: a baby bonnet, a rattle, a rubber duckie. Lorna sees Huey.

Lorna: (calling to Huey): Hi, cutie-pie. Where've you been? Want to eat lunch with us?
Huey: (Trying to be cool): I don't know. Some of the cheerleaders wanted me to eat with them. (He pauses.) What the heck. I might as well give you girls the pleasure of my company.
Sara: (faking sweetness): How condescending of you.
Huey: (modestly): I try my best. Hey, what are you guys doing Saturday night? I'm gonna have a party at my house. No parents, but plenty of other stuff. (He waves his bottle.) Want to come?

The girls look uncomfortable.

Lee: Sorry. I'm baby-sitting.
Lorna: I've gotta study.
Doon: I'm going out with Josh. Somewhere else.
Huey: You mean Josh won't come, either? (He turns to Sara.) How about you, Sexy?
Sara: (choking): I have to wash my cat.
Huey: (takes a long pull on his bottle; to Sara): You don't like me, do you?
Lee: Huey, don't—
Sara: I like you fine. It's just…the way you act sometimes.
Doon: (trying to break the tension): Hey, there's Josh.
Huey: (eager to get away): Oh, I need to talk to him. See you guys later.

Josh enters as Huey runs over to him.

Huey: Josh, you've gotta help me. I'm dying over there.
Josh: What's the matter, Bud?
Huey: Okay, here's the thing. I know some of those girls like me—they tickle me under the chin and play "This Little Piggy" with me and all. But whenever I ask them to go anywhere, none of them want to go. You're in with Doon. Do they ever talk about me? What's the deal?
Josh: Well, I did hear them talking once. About you. I'm not sure you want to hear it.
Huey: (getting down on his knees and clasping his hands together): Oh, I do I do I do. *Tell* me.
Josh: Okay. They were like, um, rating the guys in the school.
Huey: They do that, too?
Josh: Not exactly the same, but kinda. And Lee brought up you…and they agreed you were kind of cute, but….
Huey: What! But what!
Josh: Well, it was like this….

Music to "Fat Baby," from Amy Grant's Age to Age *begins playing. The girls get up from their lunch and lip-synch the song. SARA takes the lead, the others sing back-up. Choreograph it with motions like the Lennon Sisters may have used in the fifties or with soft-shoe dancing. When the girls finish singing, they sit down and resume eating.*

Huey: Oh, this is worse than I thought. They think I'm like a baby?
Josh: Well, you know you've been a Christian for as long as the rest of us, but for some reason, you're still wearing diapers.
Huey: I am? (He looks down at his diaper.) Oh my gosh! I am! What am I gonna do?
Josh: Well, for starters, you could start coming to Bible study.
Huey: (whining): But that's at the same time as my favorite TV program.
Josh: (sarcastically): That *is* a dilemma.
Huey: Yeah.

Huey looks over at the girls and suddenly remembers he's wearing a diaper. He begins to pull at it.

Oh my gosh. This diaper! Do you think the girls noticed?
Josh: What are you doing? You can't just take it off. (He propels HUEY towards the exit.) Go get some decent clothes, first.
Huey: Yeah, I guess you're right. Hmmmmm, maybe I should rethink this Bible study stuff. Will the girls be there?
Josh: Yeah, they'll be there. But you're gonna get more out of it than just seeing them.
Huey: Like what?

Josh takes Huey's bottle and tosses it up in the air as they walk toward the exit.

Josh: Ever had steak?
Huey shakes his head.

© 1991 DeGarmo and Key by Gospel Light. All rights reserved. Permission to photocopy granted.

STEP 2 READ THE WORD
SELF-EVALUATION SHEET

Memory Verse: *Like newborn babies, crave pure spiritual milk, so that by it you may grow up in your salvation, now that you have tasted that the Lord is good.* 1 Peter 2:2,3

Personal Evaluation: Respond honestly to the statements below. Then score your responses. Use this evaluation to help you as you complete the Personal Journal section.

	Almost Always	Usually	Rarely
I submit to the authority of God's Word, the Bible.	❑	❑	❑
I spend time each day reading and studying the Word.	❑	❑	❑
I listen to someone teaching from the Bible at least once a week.	❑	❑	❑
When I am not sure how God wants me to act, I look in the Bible for guidance.	❑	❑	❑

Scoring

Give yourself three points for every "almost always" answer, one point for every "usually" and zero points for "rarely."

- 9-12   You are a committed disciple.
- 6-8   You are well on your way to becoming a mature, committed disciple.
- 0-5   You need to reexamine your commitment and take steps to follow through.

Personal Journal

What analogy of the Word that was presented in this session made the most sense to you: love letters, compass, mirror, guidebook, a how-to manual, watering can, food, sword? How can you personally use the Bible in this way?

What is the most likely way you would spend more time reading and studying the Bible? What goal can you set for yourself this week?

Read again the Bible Memory Verse. (See top of page.) Commit it to your memory. How do you think you need to "grow up in your salvation"? What areas will you work on this week?

I BELIEVE

© 1991 DeGarmo and Key by Gospel Light. All rights reserved. Permission to photocopy granted.

TALK SHEET: THE PROCESS OF BIBLE STUDY

Use this side of the Talk Sheet as an optional lesson outline. The reverse side of this paper may be photocopied and handed out to class members to use with the session, or if no session is planned, you may use it as a handout for class members to take home as an additional resource.

Instructions

Option 1: If you use the outline as a basis for your session, add more details by doing some personal study in the Bible and other Christian books and by reflecting on what you've learned in your own life. Prepare some discussion questions (questions that cannot be answered by a simple yes or no). Use the reverse side of the Talk Sheet as a handout, resource or take-home paper.

Option 2: You may want to use only the reverse side of this page and simply lead the class members through the worksheet, clarifying points and adding any additional thoughts and information.

Outline

I. Personal preparation
   A. Set time/place
   B. Get an idea of what/how you want to read/study. Some examples:
      1. Old Testament or New Testament
      2. Chronological
      3. Character study
      4. Thematic/topical study
      5. Short New Testament books
      6. Life of Christ
   C. List questions, matters where you need guidance, etc.
   D. Approach with pure, humble heart (see James 1:21)
   E. Pray—confess sins, prepare to listen to the Master

II. Methods
   A. See the 3-Track Reading Plan—introduction to *The NIV Student Bible*
   B. Develop method of marking Bible
   C. Keep notes
   D. Paraphrase (write in own words) key passages to deepen understanding
   E. Note things you don't understand and research them

III. Tools (bring some examples to class)
   A. Personal notebook/journal
   B. Study Bibles or Bibles with helps (*The NIV Student Bible, NIV Study Bible, Disciple's Study Bible*, etc.)
   C. Concordances
   D. Topical indexes
   E. Bible dictionaries
   F. Commentaries

PERSONAL PREPARATION

At what time will you do your daily Bible study? Where will you study? Do you want to study a topic for a week? month? season? (Circle one.)	Check a topic you want to study: ❏ characters (e.g. David, Joshua, etc.) ❏ topics (e.g. war, prophecy, etc.) ❏ certain Bible books (e.g. short New Testament books) ❏ the life of Christ ❏ Paul's letters	What do you feel you need to study? In what situations do you need guidance? What would you like to know more about? 1. 2. 3.	What sins do you need to confess before spending time with God and His Word?	Pray that God will prepare your heart to listen and learn from His Word.

METHODS TO USE

See the 3-Track Reading Plan in *The NIV Student Bible*. Which track will you use? If you use Track 1, which track course will you use first?	Here are different methods of marking your Bible. Check the ones you hope to use: ❏ highlight different themes in different colors. ❏ underline instructions that apply especially to you. ❏ star verses or passages you memorize.	Paraphrase key passages. Practice by paraphrasing John 3:16 here:	Take notes in a notebook or directly in your Bible. What notes could you make on Ephesians 6:10-18?	Write down things you don't understand. Research them by reading or talking to spiritually mature Christians. Ask questions. For example, using Philippians 1:1— Who is Paul? Who is Timothy? Where is Philippi? Why is Paul writing? What is a deacon?

TOOLS

A personal notebook or journal in which you write down: ● What you learned ● How you can apply it to your life ● Questions. What else might you write?	Here some Bibles to help you in your studies: ● *The NIV Student Bible* ● *The NIV Study Bible* ● *Disciple's Study Bible* What Bibles are available to you?	Concordances list key words from Scripture and tell you where to find verses in which they're used. Topical indexes tell verses that go with topics. Bible dictionaries give definitions of words used in the Bible. Which do you think would be most helpful to your study?	Commentaries delve into books or subjects found in the Bible and give added insight and knowledge. Where can you get a commentary for your personal use: church library? bookstore? friend?	Books to help you through: ● *90 Days Through the New Testament* ● *What the Bible Is All About* _____ _____ _____ _____ _____

© 1991 DeGarmo and Key by Gospel Light. All rights reserved. Permission to photocopy **granted**.

GO TO THE TOP

Chorus:
You've got to
go to the top
when you need to get things done.
Go to the top
to the Father through the Son.
Go to the top.

What makes a believer
different from others around?
What gives us confidence
to look up when others look down?
Faith is really knowing
our Father provides all our needs.
Our difference is Jesus,
we have asked and we have received.

(chorus)

Some people lie down
the world beats them black and blue,
down and defeated
instead of marching on,
they withdrew.
Don't be disheartened,
the Lord hears your every prayer.
He'll answer His children,
in hard times He will be there.

(chorus)

(bridge)

At the top He sees it all.
At the top He knows what's best.
All you need to do is call
His name, call His name.

STEP 3   GO TO THE TOP

Theme: Prayer is as important to spiritual life as breath is to physical life.

Memory Verse: *Do not be anxious about anything, but in everything, by prayer and petition, with thanksgiving, present your requests to God. And the peace of God, which transcends all understanding, will guard your hearts and your minds in Christ Jesus.* Philippians 4:6,7

Checklist
You and your students will know that you have accomplished the goals of this Bible study session if:
- ❏ You understand what prayer is.
- ❏ You exercise your "total access" to God by praying daily.
- ❏ You are committed to keeping a prayer list or journal.
- ❏ You have—or have made a commitment to find—a prayer partner or a prayer group.

© 1991 DKB Music/ASCAP. All rights reserved. Used by permission. Permission to photocopy granted.

Materials
- Bibles;
- Paper and pencils or pens;
- Photocopies of the lyrics to "Go to the Top," the student worksheet and the "Self-Evaluation Sheet" for each student;
- Chalkboard or overhead projector with transparencies;

Optional
- The album *Go to the Top* by DeGarmo and Key (available at most Christian bookstores).

GO TO THE TOP

(chorus)
You've got to
go to the top
when you need to get things done.
Go to the top
to the Father through the Son.
Go to the top.

What makes a believer
different from others around?
What gives us confidence
to look up when others look down?
Faith is really knowing
our Father provides all our needs.
Our difference is Jesus,
we have asked and we have received.

(chorus)

Some people lie down
the world beats them black and blue,
down and defeated
instead of marching on,
they withdrew.
Don't be disheartened,
the Lord hears your every prayer.
He'll answer His children,
in hard times He will be there.

(chorus)

(bridge)
At the top He sees it all.
At the top He knows what's best.
All you need to do is call
His name, call His name.

© D&K Music/ASCAP. All rights reserved. Used by permission. Permission to photocopy granted.

STEP 3 — GO TO THE TOP
SELF-EVALUATION SHEET

Memory Verse: *Do not be anxious about anything, but in everything, by prayer and petition, with thanksgiving, present your requests to God. And the peace of God, which transcends all understanding, will guard your hearts and your minds in Christ Jesus.* Philippians 4:6,7

Personal Evaluation: Respond honestly to the statements below. Then score your responses. Use this evaluation to help you as you complete the Personal Journal section.

	Almost Always	Usually	Rarely
I exercise my "total access" to God by praying daily.	☐	☐	☐
I don't just ask for things in prayer. I also confess my sins, praise and thank God and pray for others.	☐	☐	☐
I have a prayer partner or prayer group that I meet with regularly.	☐	☐	☐

Scoring
Give yourself three points for every "almost always" answer, one point for every "usually" and zero points for "never."

- 9-12 You are a committed disciple.
- 6-8   You are well on your way to becoming a mature, committed disciple.
- 0-5   You need to reexamine your commitment and take steps to follow through.

Personal Journal
What new thing did you learn about prayer in this session, or what elements of prayer were you reminded of that you hadn't thought of lately?

How can you exercise total access to God more this week so that your relationship with Him will benefit you most?

Read again the Bible Memory Verse (see top of page). Commit it to your memory. What are you anxious about that you could turn over to God in prayer with thanksgiving?

© DeGarmo and Key by Gospel Light. All rights reserved. Permission to photocopy granted.

---

1 BEGIN

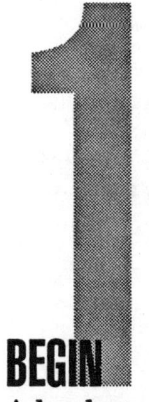

Ask volunteers, **If you could talk to anyone on earth for 30 minutes, who would it be and why would you choose that person?** Quickly jot down their answers on a piece of newsprint displayed in front of the group. Next ask, **What would you talk about?** Make note of these answers also. Finally, ask, **Who do you think is the most famous person in the whole world?** Write these names down on a separate piece of newsprint. Then say something like, **The most important Being in the whole universe is available for us to talk to any and every time we desire. Not only that, but this Person longs for each of us to spend time with Him.** Point to the names of famous people on the newsprint. Say, **These people look pretty tiny when you compare them with the Almighty Creator and Sustainer of the universe, don't they? But God, Lord of everything we can see or imagine, is the One that wants us to enjoy constant communication with Him. That's pretty awe-inspiring.**

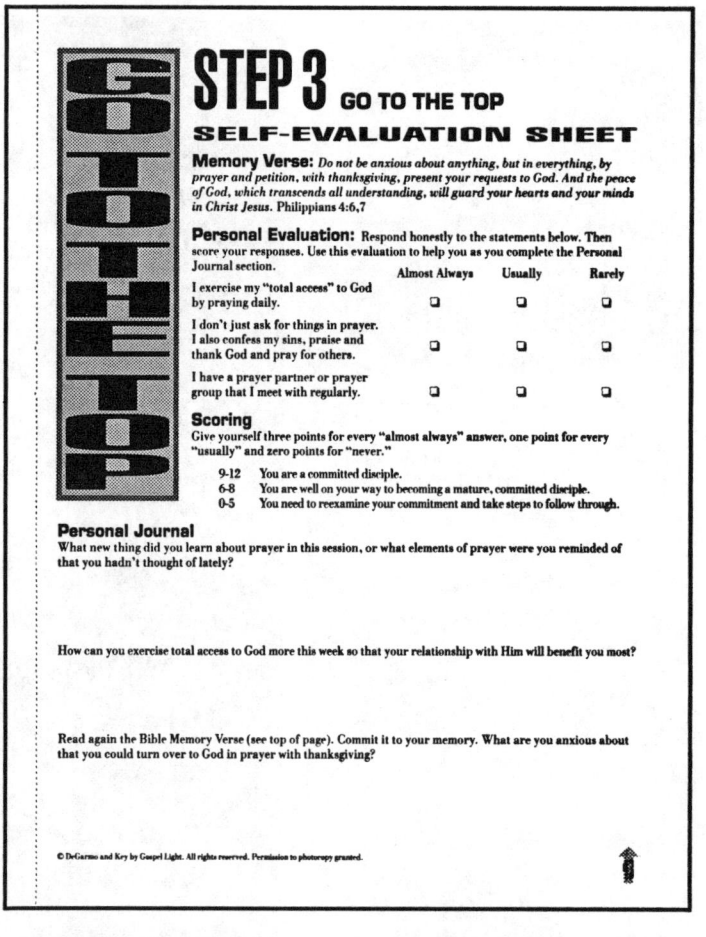

Hand out one copy of the "Go to the Top" lyrics to each student. Ask them to circle the phrases that describe or explain something about prayer.

Optional: Play the song "Go to the Top" from the album by the same title as students circle words or phrases.

After the song is over and the students are finished working, ask, **What does the phrase "Go to the top" usually mean?** The answer you are looking for is that in business, for instance, it may be hard to get what you want when you're dealing with the front people (like receptionist or maybe lower management). It's sometimes easiest to get what you want if you can talk to the boss of the whole operation. Ask, **How is the phrase "Go to the top" used in this song?** A good answer would sound something like this: The boss that they're talking about is God—He's at the very top of everything.

Write the following verses on a chalkboard or overhead projector transparency and display them:

"I will do whatever you ask in my name, so that the Son may bring glory to the Father." John 14:13

"So do not worry, saying, 'What shall we eat?' or 'What shall we drink?' or 'What shall we wear?' For the pagans run after all these things, and your heavenly Father knows that you need them. But seek first his kingdom and his righteousness, and all these things will be given to you as well." Matthew 6:31-33

"Ask and it will be given to you; seek and you will find; knock and the door will be opened to you. For everyone who asks receives; he who seeks finds; and to him who knocks, the door will be opened." Matthew 7:7,8

"The eyes of the Lord are on the righteous and his ears are attentive to their cry." Psalm 34:15

"The righteous cry out, and the Lord hears them; he delivers them from all their troubles." Psalm 34:17

"This is the confidence we have in approaching God: that if we ask anything according to his will, he hears us. And if we know that he hears us—whatever we ask—we know that we have what we asked of him." 1 John 5:14,15

Have the class members work in small groups to match these verses to phrases in the song. Tell them to write down the verses next to the phrases that seem to be speaking of similar things. After about ten minutes, regather into a larger group and go over their answers. Be flexible in the answers they chose since there are no right or wrong answers. The following answers will give you an idea of where the verses definitely *do* fit:

"through the Son"—John 14;13

"provides all our needs"—Matthew 6:31-33

"We have asked and we have received"—Matthew 7:7,8

"The Lord hears"—Psalm 34:15

"He'll answer his children"—1 John 5:14,15

"In hard times he will be there"—Psalm 34:17

Optional: Have students get into groups of three to write a short praise song using concepts from the preceding verses about prayer. Have volunteer groups write their song on the board or on transparencies and lead the group in singing the song.

2
IS PRAYER NECESSARY?

Say something like, **Just in case any of you are not convinced that prayer is a necessary part** of the Christian life, let me mention a couple of things. First, to have a relationship with anyone, you have to communicate. Prayer is how we communicate with God. And second, it's not only exciting that God wants us to talk with Him, but it's exciting that by praying, God lets us take part in His work in the world. We get to join in by praying for things that God wants to accomplish.

Ask, **Have any of you ever had prayer experiences that you especially remember? For instance, prayers answered in a remarkable way, or a real feeling that God was talking to you?** Allow plenty of time for responses and discussion. Take notes on a chalkboard or overhead transparency about the kinds of things that they talk to God about that come up in the responses. Then say, **These are some of the things that you talk about with God. What are some other things we can talk about with God?** Write those responses down also. Compare this list with the list of "What would you talk about if you could talk to anyone in the world? You may find that you need to expand the list of things to talk about with God. Have the students turn to Romans 1:9,10 and 1 John 1:9 for more ideas on things to talk to God about (intercession and confession). Make sure the following items are included in the list: talk about problems; ask for help; when feeling lonely; help with decisions; when strength is needed; when tempted; when worried about others; confessing sin.

3 JESUS' EXAMPLE

Say something like, **Let's see what we can learn from Jesus' examples of prayer.**

Ask the group to turn in their Bibles to Mark 1:35 and have a volunteer read the verse. Then say, **What does Jesus do in this example of prayer?** Write down each action or description as the class members tell them to you. Point out any they missed (early in the morning, still dark, got up, left house, went to solitary place, alone, prayed). Ask if they think any of these things, besides the actual praying, are necessary to prayer. The conclusion they should come to is that the parts of the example are not necessary to prayer, but can be a way to pray. Say, **One thing this example shows is that at times, Jesus prayed alone.**

Next, ask if anyone can think of a time when Jesus prayed with others. If no one can think of an example, have them turn to John 17. Say something like, **If you look back through chapter 16, you'll see that Jesus is talking to His disciples. Then, in chapter 17, He looks toward heaven and begins praying. This is Jesus' longest recorded prayer. We'll examine it more thoroughly later. For now, it serves as an example of a time when Jesus prayed with others.**

Have students turn to Luke 6:12,13. After a volunteer reads the passage, ask, **What do you think is significant about this example of prayer?** There are actually two acceptable answers: that Jesus prayed all night, and that He spent time talking to God before acting on an important event (or perhaps before making a major decision)—the choosing of the 12 disciples.

Say, **One of the things Jesus tells us to talk to God about is found in Matthew 9, verses 35 to 38. Read that silently to yourselves and then I'd like someone to tell me what Jesus directs us to ask God.** After a correct answer, either repeat the answer or rephrase it by saying, **One thing Jesus directs us to ask God for is workers—that God would send people who can tell others about the good news about Jesus.**

Have the class members turn to John 17. Say, **In The NIV Student Bible the editors have divided this chapter by the three different types of people that Jesus prayed for on this occasion.** Ask for a volunteer who has *The NIV Student Bible* to read the headings used in John 17. If no one has this edition, the three headings are: "Jesus Prays for Himself," "Jesus Prays for His Disciples" and "Jesus Prays for All Believers." Say, **You may want to read this chapter at home this week to learn some more about Jesus' example of prayer. This is just another example of the possible content of prayer.**

Option: Hand out a piece of paper and a pencil to each class member. Have them read John 17:20-26 silently and meditate on this prayer that Jesus prayed for them 2,000 years ago (assuming all attending are believers). They may want to write down their feelings about this prayer and what it means to them that Jesus was praying for them.

4 THE LORD'S PRAYER

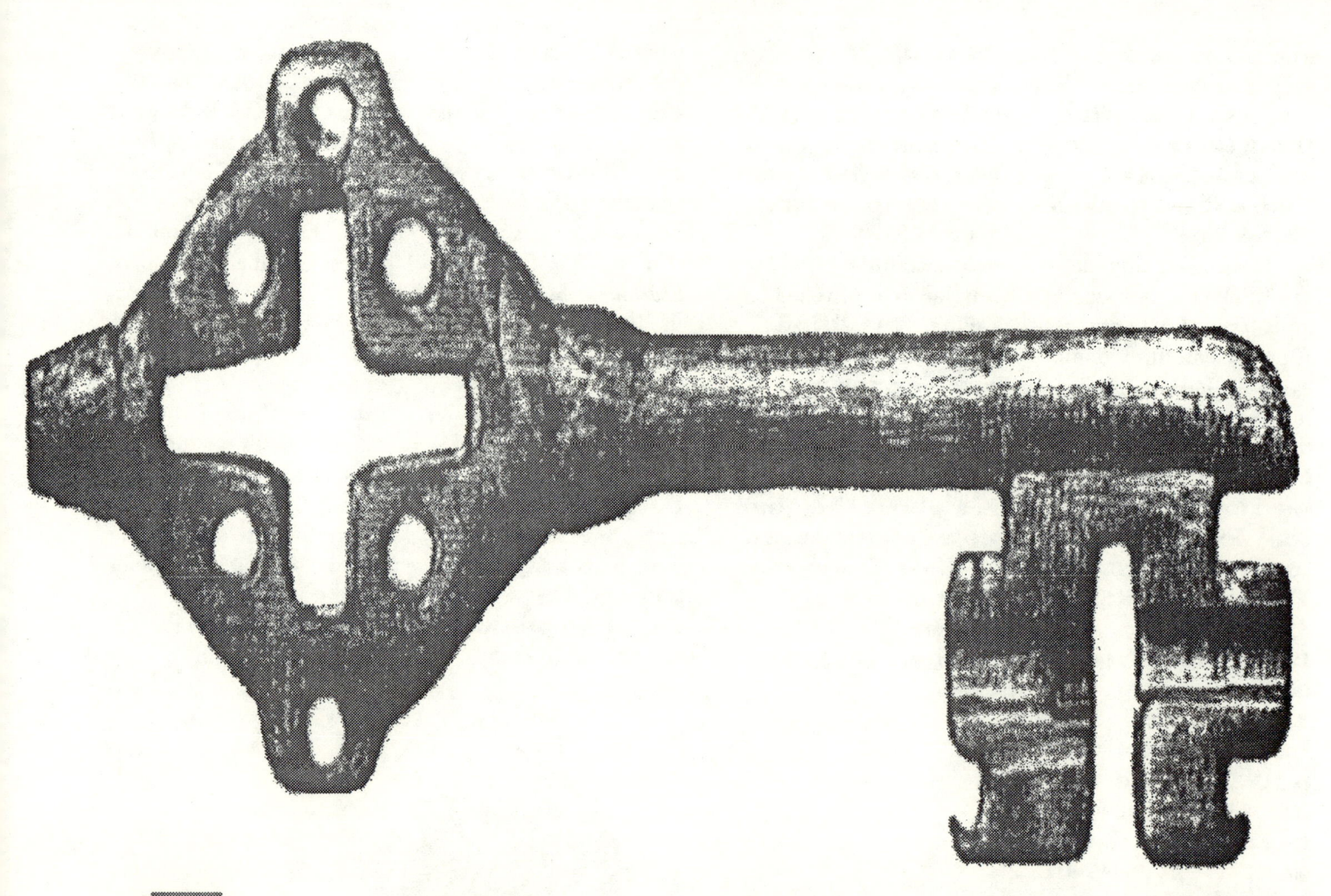

Ask the students to get into groups of two to four and turn to Matthew 6:9-13. Hand out the worksheet and explain that the students are to work on the middle column as a group and the last column by themselves. Go over the instructions with them. Be available to help the students as they need it.

5 GUIDELINES

When the students are finished working, say that you are going to go over some more guidelines about prayer from Scripture. Write on the chalkboard or overhead transparency these four questions: When is prayer effective? When is prayer not effective? How does the Spirit help in prayer? When should we pray? Assign the following Scriptures—one each to four different groups: James 4:2,3; James 5:16; 1 Thessalonians 5:17; Romans 8:26,27. As the groups find answers, one volunteer from each group should go and write their group's response on the board or transparency under the corresponding questions.

Ask if anyone would like to give an example of how to pray continually. If there is no response, you may want to direct them to 1 Thessalonians 1:3; 2:13; 5:17 and Ephesians 6:18 as further examples of constant praying. Perhaps you would like to share some experiences you have had in this attitude of prayer.

Challenge the students to try praying continually this week. Remind them that they may want to read John 17 and distribute the Self-Evaluation Sheet for students to work on at home.

Close in prayer.

Option: Suggest that class members begin a prayer journal. In the journal, they may want to write down each prayer request and the date it was requested, leaving a space for when, and how the prayer is answered.

This is a good reminder of things to pray about and a memory keeper of how God works in their lives.

GO TO THE TOP

Chorus:
You've got to
go to the top
when you need to get things done.
Go to the top
to the Father through the Son.
Go to the top.

What makes a believer
different from others around?
What gives us confidence
to look up when others look down?
Faith is really knowing
our Father provides all our needs.
Our difference is Jesus,
we have asked and we have received.

(chorus)

Some people lie down
the world beats them black and blue,
down and defeated
instead of marching on,
they withdrew.
Don't be disheartened,
the Lord hears your every prayer.
He'll answer His children,
in hard times He will be there.

(chorus)

(bridge)

At the top He sees it all.
At the top He knows what's best.
All you need to do is call
His name, call His name.

© 1991 DKB Music/ASCAP. All rights reserved. Used by permission. Permission to photocopy granted.

WORKSHEET — MATTHEW 6:9-13

THE LORD'S PRAYER AS A MODEL

Instructions: In the left column the Lord's Prayer is written out by phrases. Analyze each phrase. Then, beside each phrase (in the middle column), write the meaning of that section of the prayer. (The first one is done as an example.) After you finish analyzing the components of the prayer, complete the right-hand column by writing a prayer to God. Use the same form as the middle column, but write your prayer in your own words according to your own personal needs and feelings. Noticing these forms of prayer present in the Lord's Prayer will help you express: praise; thanksgiving; intercession; confession; petition and vows.

MODEL	MEANING	PERSONAL
Our Father in heaven,	Addressing God, who He is in relation to us, where He is	
hallowed be your name,		
your kingdom come,		
your will be done on earth as it is in heaven.		
Give us today our daily bread.		
Forgive us our debts,		
as we also have forgiven our debtors.		
And lead us not into temptation,		
but deliver us from the evil one.		

© 1991 DeGarmo and Key by Gospel Light. All rights reserved. Permission to photocopy granted.

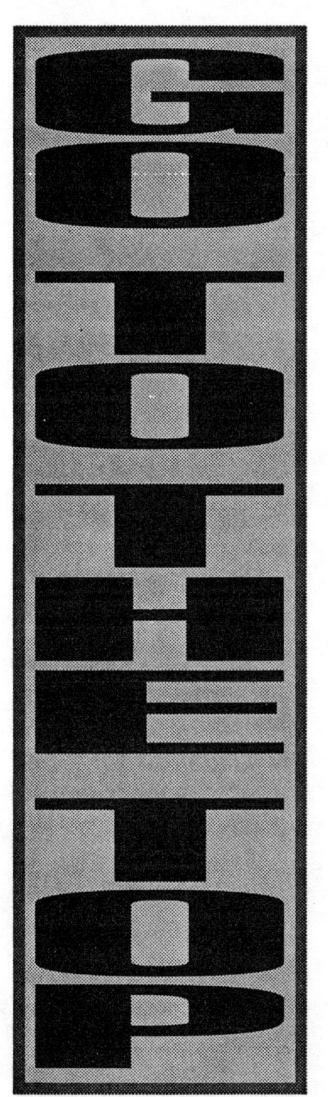

STEP 3 GO TO THE TOP
SELF-EVALUATION SHEET

Memory Verse: *Do not be anxious about anything, but in everything, by prayer and petition, with thanksgiving, present your requests to God. And the peace of God, which transcends all understanding, will guard your hearts and your minds in Christ Jesus.* Philippians 4:6,7

Personal Evaluation: Respond honestly to the statements below. Then score your responses. Use this evaluation to help you as you complete the Personal Journal section.

	Almost Always	Usually	Rarely
I exercise my "total access" to God by praying daily.	❑	❑	❑
I don't just ask for things in prayer. I also confess my sins, praise and thank God and pray for others.	❑	❑	❑
I have a prayer partner or prayer group that I meet with regularly.	❑	❑	❑

Scoring
Give yourself three points for every "almost always" answer, one point for every "usually" and zero points for "rarely."

- 9-12 You are a committed disciple.
- 6-8   You are well on your way to becoming a mature, committed disciple.
- 0-5   You need to reexamine your commitment and take steps to follow through.

Personal Journal
What new thing did you learn about prayer in this session, or what elements of prayer were you reminded of that you hadn't thought of lately?

How can you exercise total access to God more this week so that your relationship with Him will benefit you most?

Read again the Bible Memory Verse (see top of page). Commit it to your memory. What are you anxious about that you could turn over to God in prayer with thanksgiving?

© 1991 DeGarmo and Key by Gospel Light. All rights reserved. Permission to photocopy granted.

TALK SHEET: DEVELOPING A PRAYER LIFE

Use this side of the Talk Sheet as an optional lesson outline. The reverse side of this paper may be photocopied and handed out to class members to use with the session, or, if no session is planned, you may use it as a handout for class members to take home as an additional resource.

Instructions

Option 1: If you use the outline as a basis for your session, add more details by doing some personal study in the Bible and other Christian books and by reflecting on what you've learned in your own life. Prepare some discussion questions (questions that cannot be answered by a simple yes or no). Use the reverse side of the Talk Sheet as a handout, resource or take-home paper.

Option 2: You may want to use only the reverse side of this page and simply lead the class members through the worksheet, clarifying points and adding any thoughts you would like.

Outline

I. Prayer and the Christian's appeals in prayer are based on the character of Christ and the believer's position in Christ

II. Attitudes
   A. Faith (see Heb. 11:6)
   B. Humility (see Ps. 131)
   C. Sincerity or earnestness (see Jas. 5:17,18)

III. Christians should pray regularly (see Dan. 6:10,11; 1 Thess. 5:17)

IV. Hindrances to prayer
   A. Sin (see Isa. 59:1,2)
   B. Hypocrisy (see Matt. 6:5,6)
   C. Unbelief (see Matt. 17:17-21)
   D. Wrong motives (see Jas. 4:2,3)

V. How to pray
   A. Mode/What to say
   B. Posture
      1. Lifting hands and bowing down (see Neh. 8:6)
      2. Standing (see Mark 11:25)
      3. Kneeling (see Acts 20:36)
      4. Lying down (see Matt. 26:39)
      5. Real issue is not the position of the body but the condition of the heart
   C. Private prayer
   D. Group prayer
   E. Prayer partner and accountability

VI. The effects of prayer
   A. Activates God's power
   B. Aligns us with God's will

DEVELOPING A PRAYER LIFE

ATTITUDES OF PRAYER

What attitude does Hebrews 11:6 say we should have about prayer?

What attitude does Psalm 131 say we should have?

What attitude does James 5:17,18 say we should have?

We should _____ (1 Thess. 5:17)

Name some places where you might want or need to pray
1.
2.
3.

Name some times of day when you might want or need to pray.
1.
2.
3.

Name some situations in which you might want or need to pray.
1.
2.
3.

HINDRANCES TO PRAYER

Read the Scriptures below and fill in what the hindrance to prayer might be.

Isaiah 59:1,2

Name a time when this hindered your praying.

Matthew 6:5,6

Have you ever felt like a hypocrite? If yes, when?

Matthew 17:17-21

Name a time when this hindered your prayer life.

James 4:2,3

Name the last time you asked God for something with these motives in mind.

HOW TO PRAY

What things are you comfortable talking to God about?

1.
2.
3.

Write down the postures that go along with these verses:

Nehemiah 8:6

Mark 11:25

Acts 20:36

Matthew 26:39

In what posture are you most comfortable talking to God? Circle any that fit in the column to the left. Add any others here:

Write one advantage and one disadvantage of private prayer and group prayer:

PRAYER PARTNERS

Name yours, or one you wish you had:

When will or when do you get together to pray?

Are you or will you be able to be accountable to your prayer partner? Why or why not? What do you need to do to improve your accountability to your partner? What responses and attitudes might encourage your partner to be accountable to you?

© 1991 DeGarmo and Key by Gospel Light. All rights reserved. Permission to photocopy granted.

Some people are nervous about their place in life,
running on ego never satisfies.
Some aren't happy till they're king of the land;
but I don't worry 'cause I'm in God's hands.
Say amen, say amen, amen.

Chorus:
He's the Master, I'm the servant;
He's the King, and I'm the subject.
He's the Ultimate Ruler of it all.

Some got a problem with a higher force,
they answer to no one on a selfish course.
That's not for me and I'm proud to say
God rules today, just like yesterday.
Say amen, say amen, amen.

(chorus)

STEP 4 ULTIMATE RULER

Theme: Recognizing your position in Christ is the key to a productive Christian life.

Memory Verse: *I am the vine; you are the branches. If a man remains in me and I in him, he will bear much fruit; apart from me you can do nothing.* John 15:5

Checklist
You and your students will know that you have accomplished the goals of this Bible study session if:
- ❏ You have decided to serve Christ.
- ❏ You have asked the Lord to help you recognize your attitudes and actions that do not honor Him.
- ❏ You have made a commitment to change those things that need changing.
- ❏ You will be accountable to another Christian as you work on those changes.
- ❏ You have asked the Lord to make your life bear fruit for Him.

Materials
- Bibles;
- Paper and pens or pencils;
- A photocopy of the lyrics to "Ultimate Ruler" and the Step 4 Self-Evaluation Sheet for each student;
- Chalkboard and chalk or overhead transparencies and projector;

Optional
- The album *Go to the Top* by DeGarmo and Key (available at most Christian bookstores).

© 1991 DKB Music/ASCAP. All rights reserved. Used by permission. Permission to photocopy granted.

ULTIMATE RULER

Some people are nervous about their place in life,
running on ego never satisfies.
Some aren't happy till they're king of the land;
but I don't worry 'cause I'm in God's hands.
Say amen, say amen, amen.

(chorus)
He's the Master, I'm the servant;
He's the King, and I'm the subject.
He's the Ultimate Ruler of it all.

Some got a problem with a higher force,
they answer to no one on a selfish course.
That's not for me and I'm proud to say
God rules today, just like yesterday.
Say amen, say amen, amen.

(chorus)

© D&B Music/ASCAP. All rights reserved. Used by permission. Permission to photocopy granted.

1 BEGIN

Hand out the lyrics to "Ultimate Ruler." Then tell the class members that they are to kneel facing their chairs (placing the lyrics on their chairs so that they can read the words). Tell them that the kneeling position will be a symbol of their relationship with God.

Optional: Play the song "Ultimate Ruler" while they are in the kneeling position.

When the song is over, ask class members to sit in their chairs and ask them how it felt to kneel. If the students are not from a kneeling tradition, ask them if they ever knelt before God at any other time. Encourage discussion on how it feels to be in this or any other humbling position. Do they dislike it? Why or why not? Is it an uncomfortable feeling, and if so, why do they think so?

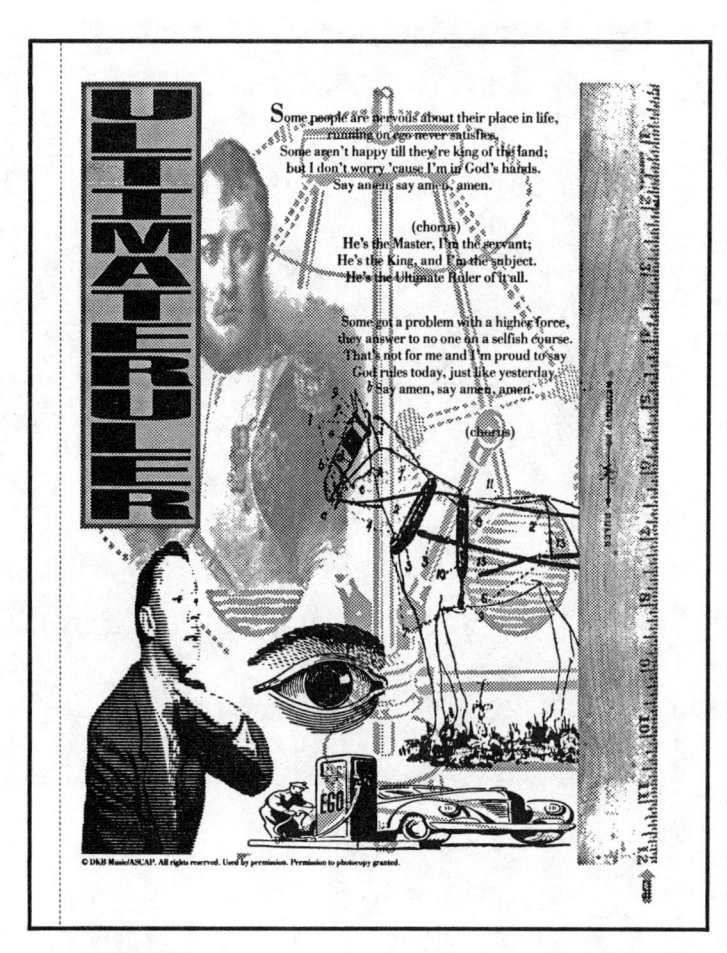

2 WHO'S ON FIRST?

Direct students' attention back to the song. Have them point out the phrases that relate to people wanting to be their own lords. Say something like, **Westerners, especially North Americans, are taught that "rugged individualism" or "being your own man" (or woman) is the way to be.** Ask someone to explain that philosophy. If no one can, say, **This philosophy says, like the song mentions, that it's best not to have to answer to anyone.** Ask, **How is this different from the Christian life?** Add to a correct answer or no answer, **Christians have to rise above this philosophy that may be ingrained in us. We must answer to Someone. We have the privilege of serving the true Master of the Universe.**

Optional: Turn to page 943 in *The NIV Student Bible* and have a volunteer read the insert called "The Role of a Servant." Say something like, **It's ironic that many of us won't allow ourselves to be put in a humble position, but Christ, the Lord, deliberately put Himself in a humble position although He deserved to be the most served.** Have a volunteer read John 13:12-17. Say, **Jesus modeled for us the role of a servant.**

3 WHAT IS LIFE?

Ask, **What is the life work or purpose of a servant?** After a response along the lines of "to serve his master," ask if anyone knows a classic, traditional response to the question of the purpose of human life on earth. The answer you are looking for is "to glorify God and enjoy Him forever" (see 1 Pet. 2:9 and The Westminster Confession) or a similar statement. Make sure everyone knows what "glorify God" means (i.e. to give honor to God). Say something like,

Being servants of God means more than doing things for God. The very way we live our lives should bring glory to God. Ask for an example of an everyday thing that could bring honor to God. One example could be studying for a test. If a student studies to the best of her ability, knowing that the ultimate glory for her success goes to God and keeping the importance of the test in the correct perspective, this may bring glory to God.

Optional: Divide the class into small groups. Give them five minutes to make up two skits (two per group). The two skits should be examples of one everyday happening done in two different ways. One way gives glory to God, the other way does not. Some subjects you might want to use: getting ready for a date; shopping for a car; doing a chore an authority figure decreed; talking with friends. Remind class members before they begin putting together their skits that "being good" doesn't mean being stuffy. Fun skits can glorify God as well as serious skits. Have the students perform their skits for each other. You may want to open a discussion on how the actions did or did not glorify God.

Say, **One thing we may want to do is check out our motivation for doing things. For instance, I could ask myself, "Am I leading this class so that I can get attention, or so that God can get attention?"** Ask for a volunteer to read Galatians 1:10. Say, **Here's a definition of what a servant is not: A servant of God is not someone who tries to please people instead of God** (see also John 12:42-43).

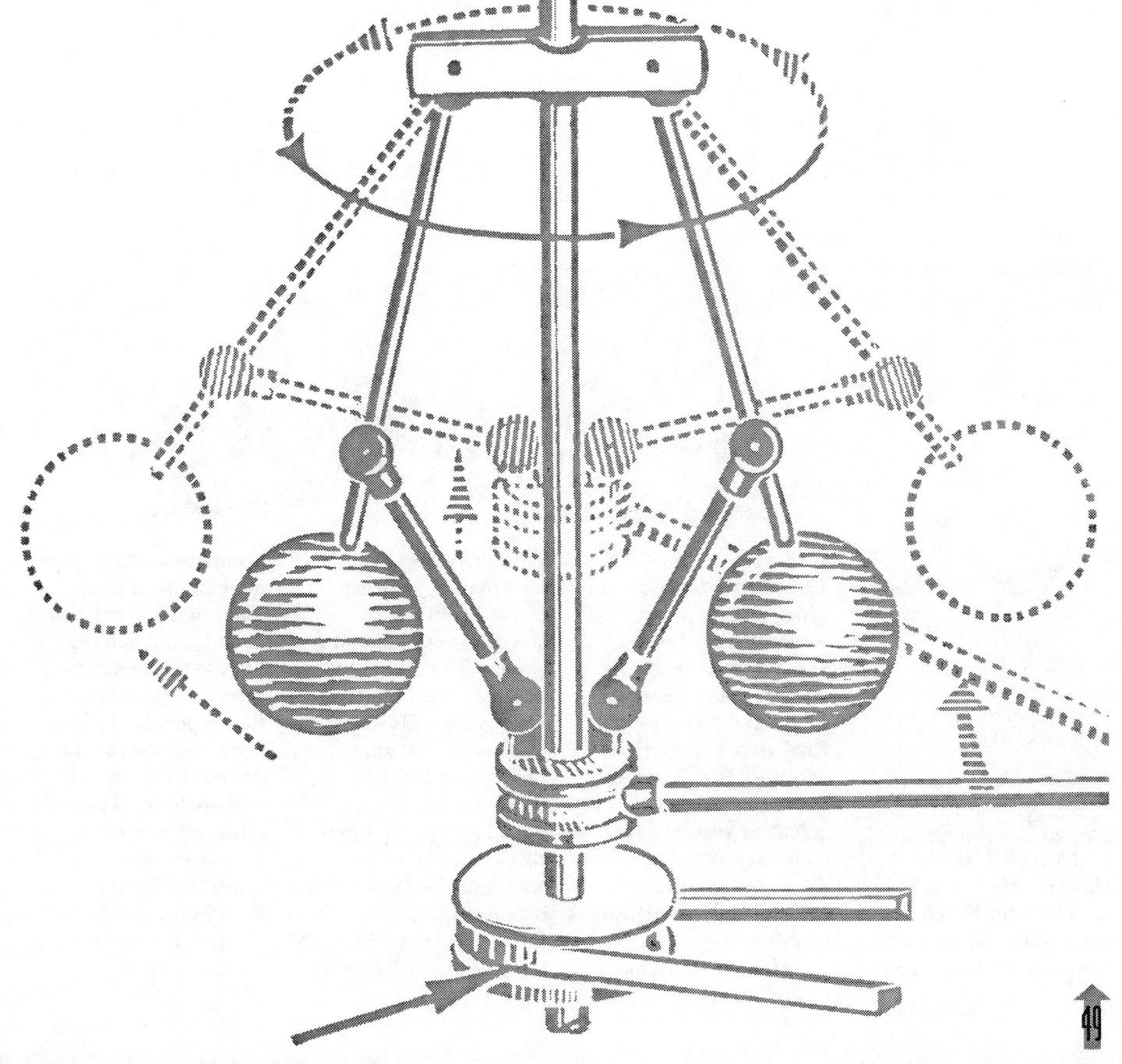

4
BEARING FRUIT

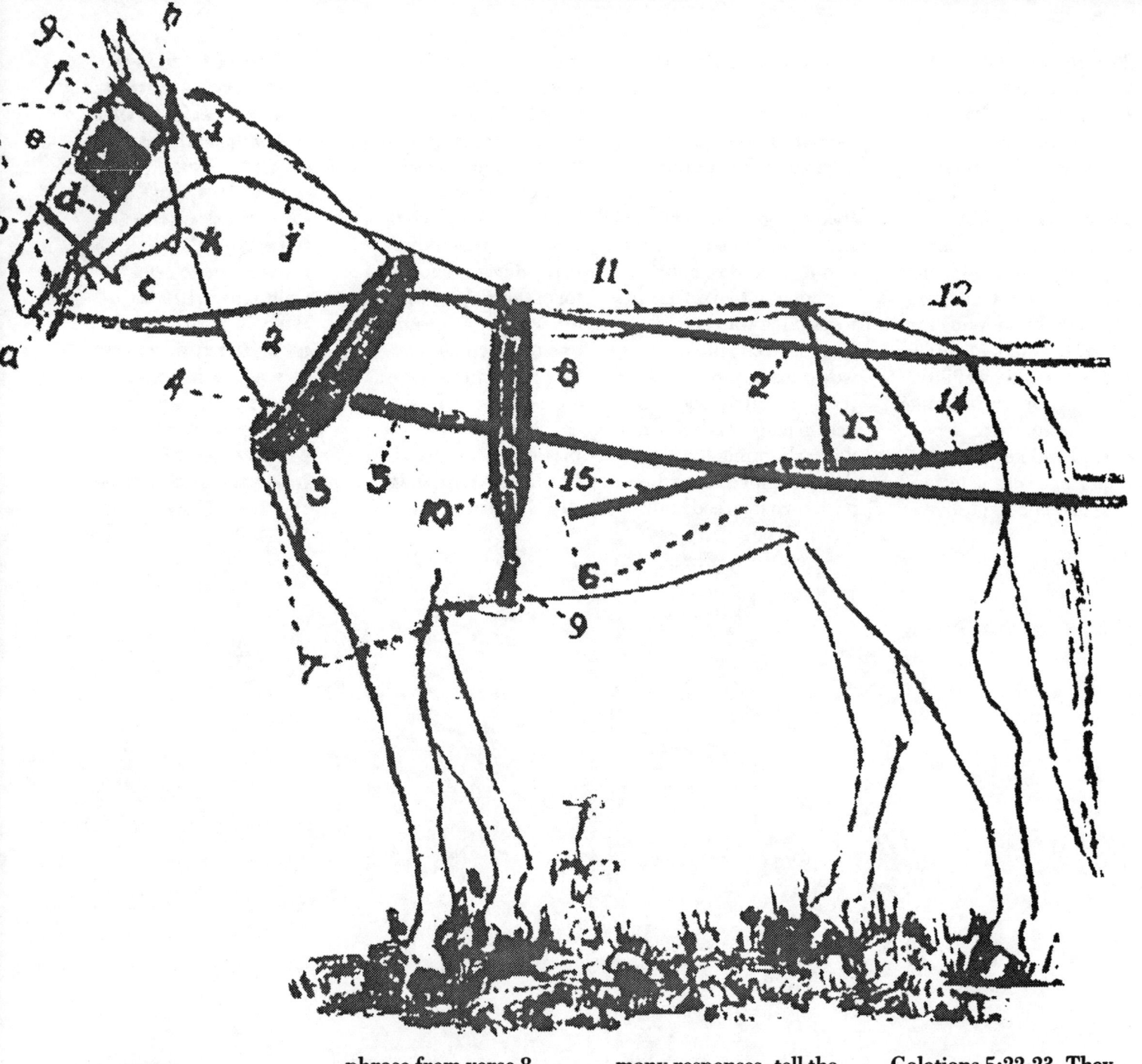

Have the class members turn to John 15:5-8. Ask for a volunteer to read the passage. Then paraphrase from verse 8. **This is to God's glory, that you bear much fruit.** Say, **So one way we can glorify God is to bear fruit. Let's find out what that means. First, can anyone tell me what it means to bear fruit?** Write down responses on a chalkboard or overhead transparency.

After encouraging many responses, tell the class that they will get into small groups to investigate examples of bearing fruit in the Bible. Split the class into four small groups. Have the first group look up Philippians 1:11 and Romans 1:13. The second should look up Matthew 28:19 and Philippians 4:17. The third—Hebrews 13:15 and Colossians 1:10. The fourth group will look up Galatians 5:22,23. They are to find out what kinds of fruit are being talked about and report back to the larger group after a few minutes. As they report back, circle responses that are the same as those already written down. Write down any new ones. Responses should look something like this:

- Philippians 1:11—righteousness; doing right

- Romans 1:13— winning converts
- Matthew 28:19— making disciples
- Philippians 4:17— giving
- Hebrews 13:15— worship; praising God
- Colossians 1:10— good works
- Galatians 5:22,23— Christlike attitudes

Say something like, **This might make you think, Do I have to bear a certain number of fruit to make it into heaven? What would you answer?** After any response, have class members turn to Ephesians 2:8,9 and ask a volunteer to read the passage. Then say, **Bearing fruit isn't something we do in order to be saved; it's something we do as a result of being saved. Just like a tree bears fruit because it is given sunlight and rain and soil, we bear fruit because we have been given the gift of Jesus Christ.**

Have another volunteer read verse 10. Ask, **What can we learn from this verse?** They should be able to come up with at least two points: we were created to bear fruit (do good works); God has prepared the works in advance for us. Say, **According to this verse, God isn't sitting and waiting for us to bear fruit by ourselves. God has prepared the works in advance for us. Let's take a look at a couple more verses on this subject.** Have class members turn to Philippians 1:6 and 2:13. After volunteers read the verses, ask what can be learned from them. Points that should come out are: God begins the work in us; God will continue the work He began in us until it is completed; God works on our intentions and our actions; goal—God's will is done.

Say, **Let's look at one more way the Bible uses the analogy of bearing fruit. Turn to John 15.** Have a volunteer read verses 1 and 2. Add, **If we bear fruit, we will be pruned. What do you think Jesus meant by that? First, tell me what happens when a tree is pruned.**

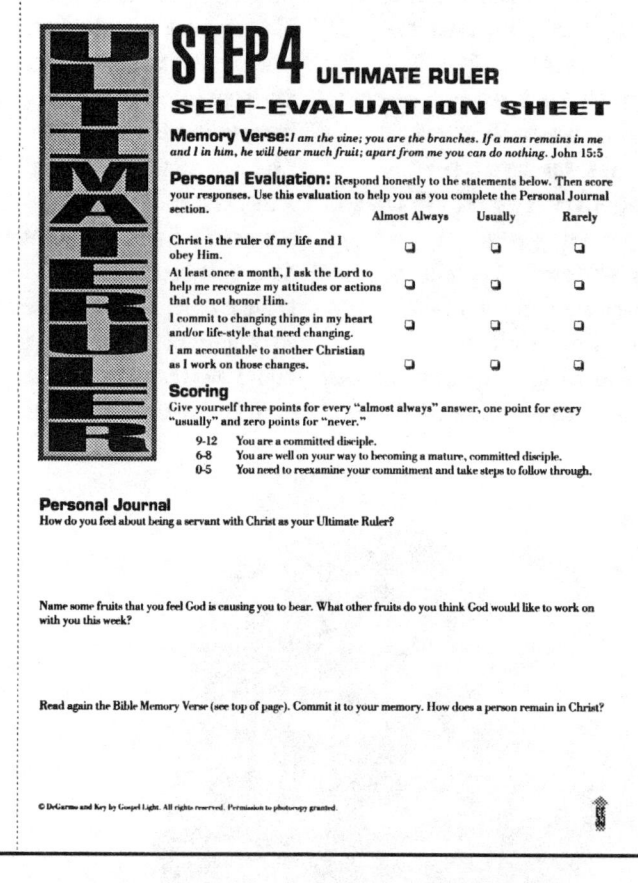

STEP 4 ULTIMATE RULER
SELF-EVALUATION SHEET

Memory Verse: *I am the vine; you are the branches. If a man remains in me and I in him, he will bear much fruit; apart from me you can do nothing.* John 15:5

Personal Evaluation: Respond honestly to the statements below. Then score your responses. Use this evaluation to help you as you complete the Personal Journal section.

	Almost Always	Usually	Rarely
Christ is the ruler of my life and I obey Him.	❑	❑	❑
At least once a month, I ask the Lord to help me recognize my attitudes or actions that do not honor Him.	❑	❑	❑
I commit to changing things in my heart and/or life-style that need changing.	❑	❑	❑
I am accountable to another Christian as I work on those changes.	❑	❑	❑

Scoring
Give yourself three points for every "almost always" answer, one point for every "usually" and zero points for "never."

- 9-12 You are a committed disciple.
- 6-8 You are well on your way to becoming a mature, committed disciple.
- 0-5 You need to reexamine your commitment and take steps to follow through.

Personal Journal
How do you feel about being a servant with Christ as your Ultimate Ruler?

Name some fruits that you feel God is causing you to bear. What other fruits do you think God would like to work on with you this week?

Read again the Bible Memory Verse (see top of page). Commit it to your memory. How does a person remain in Christ?

© DeGarmo and Key by Gospel Light. All rights reserved. Permission to photocopy granted.

After responses (you may need to help out), say, **So what do you think Jesus meant by saying that God will prune us?** Answers could be: God might guide us; discipline us; ask us to give up some object or habit; do whatever it takes to make us more fruitful.

Say something like, **Let's end with what the Ultimate Ruler says about our position in Christ.** Have a volunteer read John 15:4,5.

Distribute the Self-Evaluation Sheet for students to work on at home.

Close in prayer.

Option: If you wish to have a slide show for Step 5, now would be a good time to recruit volunteers to put it together. See Step 5 session plan for more information regarding this project.

ULTIMATE RULER

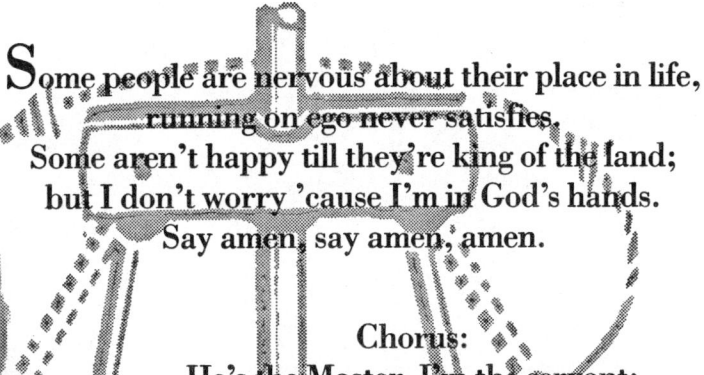

Some people are nervous about their place in life,
running on ego never satisfies.
Some aren't happy till they're king of the land;
but I don't worry 'cause I'm in God's hands.
Say amen, say amen, amen.

Chorus:
He's the Master, I'm the servant;
He's the King, and I'm the subject.
He's the Ultimate Ruler of it all.

Some got a problem with a higher force,
they answer to no one on a selfish course.
That's not for me and I'm proud to say
God rules today, just like yesterday.
Say amen, say amen, amen.

(chorus)

© 1991 DKB Music/ASCAP. All rights reserved. Used by permission. Permission to photocopy granted.

STEP 4 ULTIMATE RULER
SELF-EVALUATION SHEET

Memory Verse: *I am the vine; you are the branches. If a man remains in me and I in him, he will bear much fruit; apart from me you can do nothing.* John 15:5

Personal Evaluation: Respond honestly to the statements below. Then score your responses. Use this evaluation to help you as you complete the Personal Journal section.

	Almost Always	Usually	Rarely
Christ is the ruler of my life and I obey Him.	☐	☐	☐
At least once a month, I ask the Lord to help me recognize my attitudes or actions that do not honor Him.	☐	☐	☐
I commit to changing things in my heart and/or life-style that need changing.	☐	☐	☐
I am accountable to another Christian as I work on those changes.	☐	☐	☐

Scoring
Give yourself three points for every "almost always" answer, one point for every "usually" and zero points for "rarely."

- 9-12   You are a committed disciple.
- 6-8   You are well on your way to becoming a mature, committed disciple.
- 0-5   You need to reexamine your commitment and take steps to follow through.

Personal Journal
How do you feel about being a servant with Christ as your Ultimate Ruler?

Name some fruits that you feel God is causing you to bear. What other fruits do you think God would like to work on with you this week?

Read again the Bible Memory Verse (see top of page). Commit it to your memory. How does a person remain in Christ?

© 1991 DeGarmo and Key by Gospel Light. All rights reserved. Permission to photocopy granted.

TALK SHEET: THE FRUIT OF THE SPIRIT

Use this side of the Talk Sheet as an optional lesson outline. The reverse side of this paper may be photocopied and handed out to class members to use with the session, or if no session is planned, you may use it as a handout for class members to take home as an additional resource to the basic session Step 4—Ultimate Ruler.

Instructions

Option 1: If you use the outline as a basis for your session, add more details by doing some personal study in the Bible and other Christian books and by reflecting on what you've learned in your own life. Prepare some discussion questions (questions that cannot be answered by a simple yes or no). Use the reverse side of the Talk Sheet as a handout, resource or take-home paper.

Option 2: You may want to use only the reverse side of this page and simply lead the class members through the worksheet, clarifying points and adding any thoughts you would like.

Outline

I. Galatians 5:22,23—this passage refers to "attitude" spiritual fruit

II. Right actions follow right attitudes
   A. We can practice right attitudes or discipline ourselves in right attitudes. "Dress up like Christ," as C.S. Lewis said.
   B. Let the Spirit lead you (Galatians 5:16-18)
   C. Beware of legalism—right actions with wrong motives

III. Galatians 5:19-26—contrast these acts of a sinful nature with the fruit of the Spirit
   A. Define all the listed sinful acts
   B. Acts of sinful nature also begin with attitudes—wrong ones
      1. Matthew 5:28
      2. Matthew 12:34,35

THE FRUIT OF THE SPIRIT

READ GALATIANS 5:22,23

Write down one fruit of the Spirit next to each number	In this column, write a definition of each fruit
1.	
2.	
3.	
4.	
5.	
6.	
7.	
8.	
9.	

The fruit of the Spirit refers to attitudes that indicate the state of your heart. Examine the state of your heart by reviewing how well you are doing with each fruit of the Spirit.

List the fruit. Circle those you feel you need to work on the most. Make notes concerning how you feel you are doing with each fruit.

1.
2.
3.
4.
5.
6.
7.
8.
9.

C.S. Lewis has said that if we "dress up like Christ," or practice having the right attitudes, we will become more like Him not only in action, but also in heart attitude. How can you dress up like Christ this week?

READ GALATIANS 5:16,18

What do you think it means to be led by the Spirit?

READ GALATIANS 5:19-26

Write down one act of sinful nature next to each number	In this column write a definition of each act of the sinful nature:
1.	
2.	
3.	
4.	
5.	
6.	
7.	
8.	
9.	
10.	
11.	
12.	
13.	
14.	
15.	

READ MATTHEW 5:27,28 AND MATTHEW 12:34

The acts of sinful nature also begin with attitudes and indicate the state of your heart. Examine the state of your heart by reviewing how well you avoid these sinful acts.

List the sinful acts. Circle the ones that are hardest for you to avoid. Note also how you act when you are confronted with these temptations.

1.
2.
3.
4.
5.
6.
7.
8.
9.
10.
11.
12.
13.
14.
15.

How do you think God feels when people do the right actions but for the wrong motives?

What are some wrong motives?

© 1991 DeGarmo and Key by Gospel Light. All rights reserved. Permission to photocopy granted.

FAMILY REUNION

Far away in the distance
a candle burns for me.
Here's a prayer that's being said
by someone I've never seen.
A simple prayer for believers
that they will be okay.
It's God's love that motivates
a stranger's heart to pray.

Chorus:
It's gonna be a family reunion
when we see the Lord.
At the family reunion
we'll be home for evermore.

So diverse are the faces
in the family of God,
you can know that others walked
the road you are on.
It is good we can share
and let our burdens go.
A true friend is one that cares,
your love's worth more than gold.

(chorus)

STEP 5 FAMILY REUNION

Theme: In fellowship with other Christians, believers can be encouraged, receive instruction and be equipped for ministry.

Memory Verse: *Let the word of Christ dwell in you richly as you teach and admonish one another with all wisdom, and as you sing psalms, hymns and spiritual songs with gratitude in your hearts to God.* Colossians 3:16

Checklist

You and your students will know you have accomplished the goals of this Bible study session if:
- ❏ You seek to live at peace with other believers.
- ❏ You meet regularly with other believers for worship and to receive instruction and encouragement.
- ❏ You confess your sins to each other and pray for one another.
- ❏ You look for ways to minister to the needs of Christian brothers and sisters.

Materials
- Bibles;
- Paper and pencils or pens;
- A photocopy of the lyrics to "Family Reunion" and the Step 5 Self-Evaluation Sheet for each participant;
- Chalkboard or overhead projector and transparencies;

© 1991 DKB Music/ASCAP. All rights reserved. Used by permission. Permission to photocopy granted.

Optional
- An assortment of art supplies, for example: poster board, watercolor paper, watercolors, poster paints, brushes, marking pens, magazines, scissors, pastel chalk;
- The album, *Go to the Top*;
- Slide projector and slide show;
- The video, *The Pledge*, with TV and VCR.

Preparation: If you will be using the optional slide show, put together or have volunteers put together slides that go with the song "Family Reunion." Besides choosing slides that go along with the lyrics, slides used should be of class members, church activity or youth groups, people from the church working in service projects or possibly on mission trips; missionaries supported by the church or by the class.

1 BEGIN

Hand out the lyrics to "Family Reunion." If you have the album, play the song while students follow along with the lyrics.

Optional: While the music plays, present the slide show.

Ask, **Who are DeGarmo and Key speaking of when they say "family" in this song?** Some correct answers would be: family of God, Body of Christ, believers, Christians, the Church.

? WHAT IS THE CHURCH?

Optional: Say something like, **Because the Bible uses so many colorful pictures of what the Church, or family of God is, today we're going to be artistic.**

Explain that they are to get in groups of no more than three. If some people take art very seriously and want to create by themselves, allow that. Make sure that each of the following scriptural passages is worked on (depending on the number of your groups, you may need to double some assignments): John 1:12; John 10:14; John 15:5; John 18:36,37; Ephesians 5:22-33; Colossians 1:18.

Class members are to read the assigned passage, then depict the Church as the passage describes, interpreting it through their artistic endeavors. They may use any art medium that is available. Let them know beforehand that they will be sharing their work with the class when everyone is finished. Encourage them to think about any deeper meaning they can come up with, and to add that to their work. Give plenty of time to work, then regather into a larger group and have class members take turns explaining what they have done and why.

If you don't use the art project, divide the class into small groups and assign one or two of the same verses to each group (John 1:12; John 10:14; John 15:5; John 18:36,37; Ephesians 5:22-33; Colossians 1:18). Hand out paper and pencils or pens. The students are to read the passages, then discuss in their groups all the ideas they can come up with that might give the analogy meaning. For instance, if they are considering the depiction of the Church as a flock of sheep, they might think of the following:
- the Church's helplessness without Christ;
- the Christian's recognition of the Shepherd's voice;
- the trust the sheep have in the Shepherd;
- the protection of the Shepherd.

(Study Bibles and Bible dictionaries would be excellent resources to use.)

After everyone has completed the assignment, have class members take turns sharing their passage and the insights they discussed in their groups. Allow time for further discussion and for members of other groups to share any extra insights they may have.

Direct class members' attention back to the lyrics of "Family Reunion." Ask, **What do you think of when you hear the word, "family"?** Unless you have an unusual class, you will probably hear some negative comments about the word. Allow for some vented feelings and allow for others who don't have negative feelings to help share what a good family is all about. Ask, **What are some characteristics of a good family?** You may want to say, **If you feel your family is not a good model of what a family should be, think of another family—either one you know or imagine, one you may wish you were part of.** Write the characteristics of a good family as students share their ideas. These may include: cares for its members; members accept each other; they encourage and exhort one another; are honest with each other; work on problems together; share; etc.

3 SOLVING CONFLICTS

Then say, **Because families, including the family of God, are made up of people who are not perfect, there are bound to be conflicts. But we are called to live at peace with each other.** Have students turn to Romans 12:16-18. Ask for a volunteer to read the passage.

Say, **The Bible gives some examples of the early church's conflicts. We're going to get into small groups to discover what the problems seemed to be and Paul's advice concerning these conflicts.** Divide the class into three small groups. Group one will look at

Romans 15:5-7, group two at 1 Corinthians 1:10-13 and group three will examine Philippians 2:1-4 and 4:2,3. Advise the students that they may need to read Scriptures before or after their assigned verses to determine the possible conflict.

Regather into the larger group and put the following two headings on the chalkboard or an overhead transparency: The Conflict; Paul's Advice. Ask each group to report on what they learned from their passage. Write the information down under the corresponding heading.

Say something like, **Because Paul was a kind of father to the early church, he had a lot of advice for these early Christians concerning their behavior toward each other. Let's look at some more advice he gave.** Tell the students that you'd like to have them think of incidents in their lives that may relate to the advice Paul gave in the passages you read. Have them turn to Matthew 18:15-17. Ask a volunteer to read the passage. Then say, **Think of a situation where this advice might have worked better than the solution that was used.**

Have students turn to James 5:16. After a volunteer reads, say, **Are you able to confess your sins to someone in the family of God? You don't need to answer yes or no to that question, but could someone tell me how confession of sins might be helpful in a believer's life?** Points that should be brought out are: the burden is shared; the person confessed to can help by praying for the person who confessed; the person told can hold the person who confessed responsible for future actions and exhort him or her to avoid temptation.

Ask the class members to turn to 1 Thessalonians 5:11 and have a volunteer read. Say, **Think about who in the past could have benefited from your encouragement.**

Who needs your encouragement today?

Next, direct attention to Galatians 6:2. After a volunteer reads, ask, **Are some of you carrying burdens that the rest of us could help you carry?** If this does not spark discussion, or if class members do not want to make themselves vulnerable by answering the question, say something like, **We as believers need to become sensitive to the needs of others so that we can help carry each other's burdens,** and move on.

Optional: Cue the video *The Pledge* to the song "Hand in Hand" and play that segment for the class. Ask for a few responses to the presentation.

4 WORSHIPING TOGETHER

Direct attention to Acts 2:42-47, and have volunteers take turns reading the verses. Say, **One thing the family of God does is worship together. For the sake of those of us who have a fuzzy understanding of what worship is, let's make a list of the elements that are included and see if we can figure out a definition from that.**

Let the class brainstorm things that are included in worship. Write their ideas on a chalkboard or overhead transparency. Help to spur thoughts by referring to the passage just read in Acts and to Matthew 18:19,20; Ephesians 5:19; Colossians 3:16,17; and Revelation 4:8-11. Some things you may want to make sure are included are: an outward demonstration of honoring God; encouraging each other; motivating each other; increasing love for each other; guaranteeing God's presence; creating unity; publicly confessing Christ; being edified by the teaching of the Word; giving thanks and praise to God.

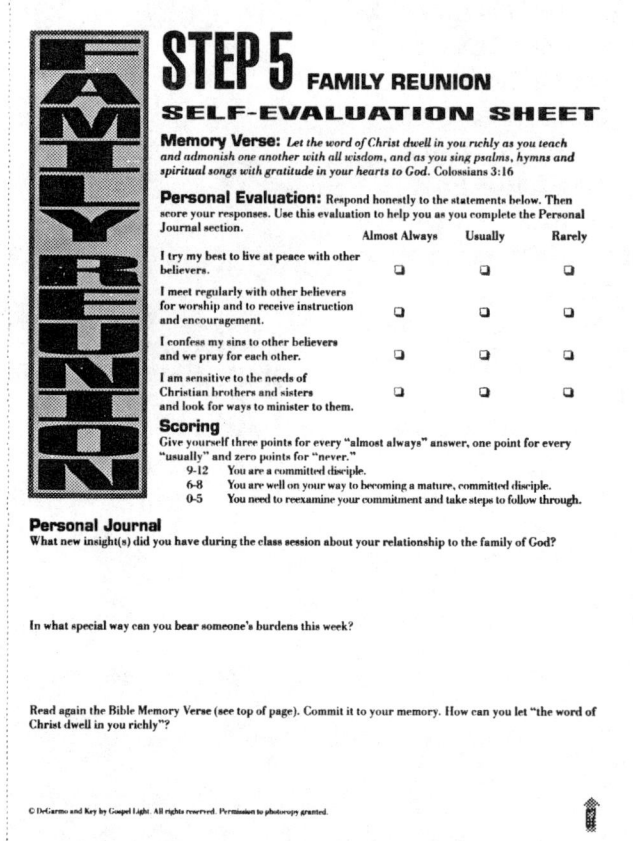

You may want to use the brainstorming sheet as an "unmolded" definition.

Optional: For an interesting essay on the role of music in worship, you may want to read aloud "Lyrics for the Living God," from *The NIV Student Bible*, found in the front of this coursebook (reprinted by permission of Zondervan Bible Publishers).

Distribute the Self-Evaluation Sheet for class members to work on at home.

Close in prayer or by reading Colossians 3:12-15.

STEP 5 FAMILY REUNION
SELF-EVALUATION SHEET

Memory Verse: *Let the word of Christ dwell in you richly as you teach and admonish one another with all wisdom, and as you sing psalms, hymns and spiritual songs with gratitude in your hearts to God. Colossians 3:16*

Personal Evaluation: Respond honestly to the statements below. Then score your responses. Use this evaluation to help you as you complete the Personal Journal section.

	Almost Always	Usually	Rarely
I try my best to live at peace with other believers.	☐	☐	☐
I meet regularly with other believers for worship and to receive instruction and encouragement.	☐	☐	☐
I confess my sins to other believers and we pray for each other.	☐	☐	☐
I am sensitive to the needs of Christian brothers and sisters and look for ways to minister to them.	☐	☐	☐

Scoring
Give yourself three points for every "almost always" answer, one point for every "usually" and zero points for "never."
- 9-12 You are a committed disciple.
- 6-8   You are well on your way to becoming a mature, committed disciple.
- 0-5   You need to reexamine your commitment and take steps to follow through.

Personal Journal
What new insight(s) did you have during the class session about your relationship to the family of God?

In what special way can you bear someone's burdens this week?

Read again the Bible Memory Verse (see top of page). Commit it to your memory. How can you let "the word of Christ dwell in you richly"?

© DeGarmo and Key by Gospel Light. All rights reserved. Permission to photocopy granted.

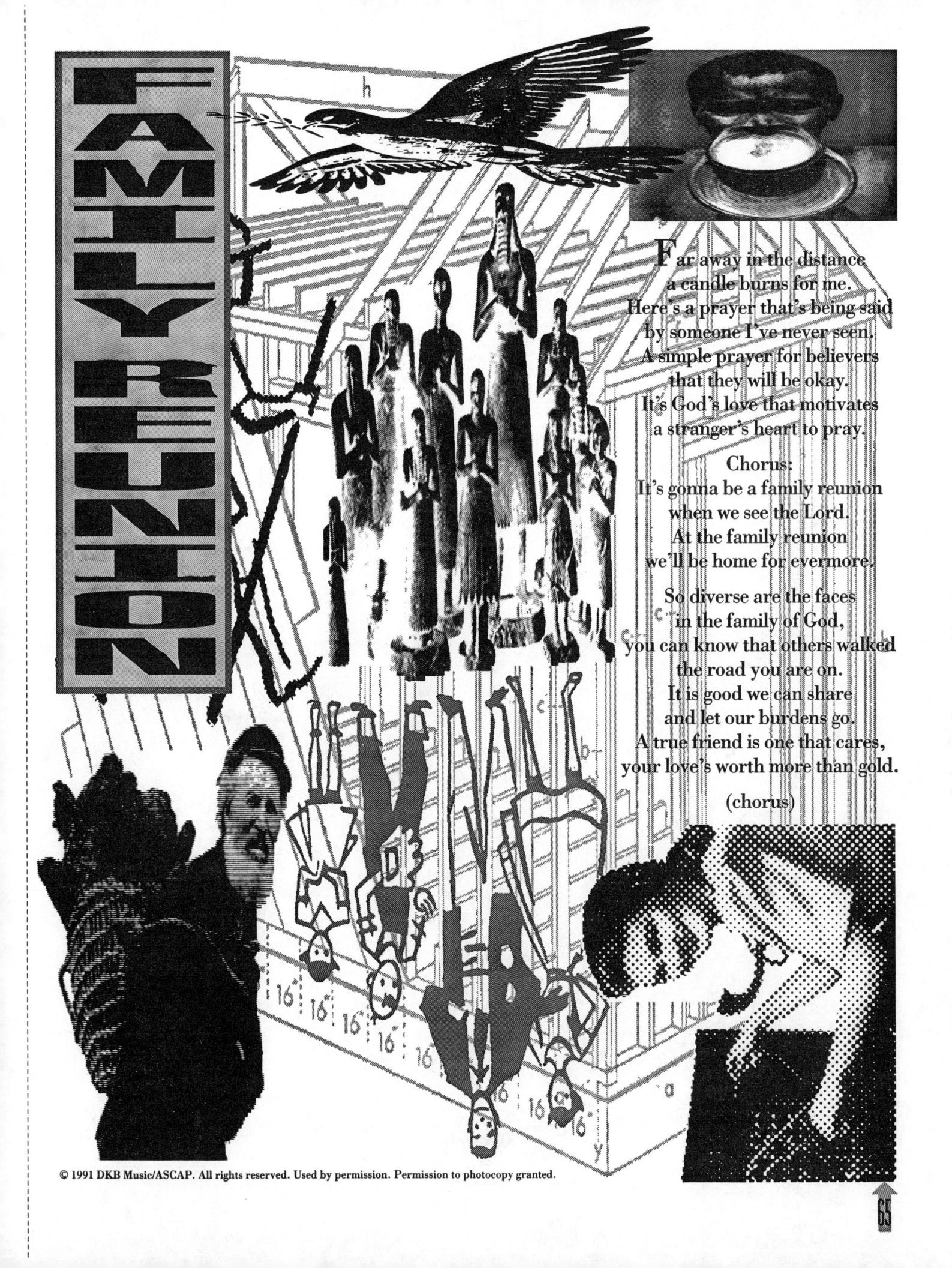

FAMILY REUNION

Far away in the distance
a candle burns for me.
Here's a prayer that's being said
by someone I've never seen.
A simple prayer for believers
that they will be okay.
It's God's love that motivates
a stranger's heart to pray.

Chorus:
It's gonna be a family reunion
when we see the Lord.
At the family reunion
we'll be home for evermore.

So diverse are the faces
in the family of God,
you can know that others walked
the road you are on.
It is good we can share
and let our burdens go.
A true friend is one that cares,
your love's worth more than gold.

(chorus)

© 1991 DKB Music/ASCAP. All rights reserved. Used by permission. Permission to photocopy granted.

STEP 5 FAMILY REUNION
SELF-EVALUATION SHEET

Memory Verse: *Let the word of Christ dwell in you richly as you teach and admonish one another with all wisdom, and as you sing psalms, hymns and spiritual songs with gratitude in your hearts to God.* Colossians 3:16

Personal Evaluation: Respond honestly to the statements below. Then score your responses. Use this evaluation to help you as you complete the Personal Journal section.

	Almost Always	Usually	Rarely
I try my best to live at peace with other believers.	❑	❑	❑
I meet regularly with other believers for worship and to receive instruction and encouragement.	❑	❑	❑
I confess my sins to other believers and we pray for each other.	❑	❑	❑
I am sensitive to the needs of Christian brothers and sisters and look for ways to minister to them.	❑	❑	❑

Scoring
Give yourself three points for every "almost always" answer, one point for every "usually" and zero points for "rarely."

- 9-12   You are a committed disciple.
- 6-8   You are well on your way to becoming a mature, committed disciple.
- 0-5   You need to reexamine your commitment and take steps to follow through.

Personal Journal
What new insight(s) did you have during the class session about your relationship to the family of God?

In what special way can you bear someone's burdens this week?

Read again the Bible Memory Verse (see top of page). Commit it to your memory. How can you let "the word of Christ dwell in you richly"?

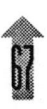

© 1991 DeGarmo and Key by Gospel Light. All rights reserved. Permission to photocopy granted.

TALK SHEET: SPIRITUAL GIFTS

Use this side of the Talk Sheet as an optional lesson outline. The reverse side of this paper may be photocopied and handed out to class members to use with the session, or if no session is planned, you may use it as a handout for class members to take home as an additional resource to the basic lesson, Step 5—Family Reunion.

Instructions

Option 1: If you use the outline as a basis for your session, add more details by doing some personal study in the Bible and other Christian books and by reflecting on what you've learned in your own life. Prepare some discussion questions (questions that cannot be answered by a simple yes or no). Use the reverse side of the Talk Sheet as a handout, resource or take-home paper.

Option 2: You may want to use only the reverse side of this page and simply lead the class members through the worksheet, clarifying points and adding any thoughts you would like.

Outline

I. What are spiritual gifts?
   A. Channel through which you can minister
   B. Source is Holy Spirit (1 Cor. 12:4-6)
   C. There are different kinds of gifts but one Spirit (1 Cor. 12:4-6)
      1. Prophecy (Rom. 12:6)
      2. Ministry, serving or helps (Rom. 12:7; 1 Cor. 12:28)
      3. Teaching (Rom. 12:7)
      4. Mercy (Rom. 12:8)
      5. Exhortation or encouraging (Rom. 12:8)
      6. Giving (Rom 12:8)
      7. Administration or leadership (Rom. 12:8)
      8. Wisdom (1 Cor. 12:8)
      9. Knowledge (1 Cor. 12:8)
      10. Faith (1 Cor. 12:9)
      11. Healing (1 Cor. 12:9,28,30)
      12. Discernment (1 Cor. 12:10)
      13. Miracles (1 Cor. 12:10,28)
      14. Tongues (1 Cor. 12:10,28)
      15. Interpretation of tongues (1 Cor. 12:10)
   D. Different fellowships' lists of gifts and how they are used in the Body may differ slightly. Ask your pastor or other leader how the gifts operate in your fellowship.

II. Purpose of gifts (Acts 14:12,26)

III. Identify and plan to use your gifts

© 1991 DeGarmo and Key by Gospel Light. All rights reserved. Permission to photocopy granted.

SPIRITUAL GIFTS

READ 1 CORINTHIANS 12:4-6 AND FILL IN THE BLANKS

There are different kinds of _____, but the same _____.

There are different kinds of _____, but the same _____.

There are different kinds of _____, but the same _____ works all of them in all men.

READ 1 CORINTHIANS 12:7. WHAT IS THE PURPOSE OF GIFTS?

Write down the gifts listed in 1 Corinthians 12:8-10.
1.
2.
3.
4.
5.
6.
7.
8.
9.

Write down the gifts listed in Romans 12:6-8. Circle any gifts that are in both lists.
1.
2.
3.
4.
5.
6.
7.

Next to each gift listed write its definition. You may get the information from your church's resources or by using a study Bible, a Bible dictionary or a commentary.

Knowing the definitions of these gifts, which do you think you may have?

Ask three Christians who know you well what they think your gifts may be.

Name: Name: Name:

Possible gifts: Possible gifts: Possible gifts:
_____   _____   _____
_____   _____   _____
_____   _____   _____
_____   _____   _____

Do any of your possible gifts show up in more than one of the above columns? If yes, which one(s)?

Do any of your possible gifts show up in all three of the columns? If yes, which one(s)?

How do the three Christians' responses compare to your ideas about your possible gifts?

Return to the list of spiritual gifts and put a star by any gifts that you think you may have according to what you have found out.

How do you think you could best use these gifts for the benefit of the Church?

© 1991 DeGarmo and Key by Gospel Light. All rights reserved. Permission to photocopy granted.

STAND, FIGHT, WIN

Behind the news in the hearts of men
there are fights to fight and wars to win.
You've heard the trumpet sound,
this is your hour.
There is a ruler in the unseen world
that is filled with hate, filled with sin.
You've got the strength to win.
Stand in His power.

Chorus:
Stand, fight, win,
You've got the power to stand;
Stand, fight, win,
This is the hour to
Stand, fight, win.
You've got to stand and fight to win.

Don't be a slave to the mundane world;
there are fights to fight, wars to win.
Awaken from your sleep and run to the battle.
Look at your world through eyes of faith,
no time to waste, emergency.
You've got all you need,
helmet to sandal.

(chorus)

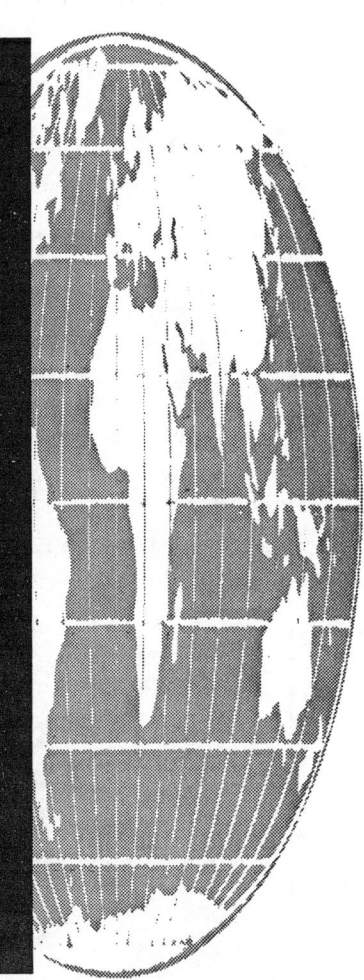

STEP 6 STAND, FIGHT, WIN

Theme: In this life Christians battle temptation and the forces of darkness.

Memory Verse: *Live as children of light (for the fruit of the light consists in all goodness, righteousness and truth) and find out what pleases the Lord. Have nothing to do with the fruitless deeds of darkness but rather expose them.* Ephesians 5:8-11

Checklist

You and your students will know that you have accomplished the goals of this Bible study session if:
- ❑ You understand the spiritual forces you battle against as a Christian.
- ❑ You know the armor and weapons God provides you to fight temptation and spiritual darkness.
- ❑ You have studied the costs and rewards of discipleship and haverea firmed your resolve to be Christ's disciple.
- ❑ When you fail, you repent and ask God for forgiveness and seek the counsel and prayers of mature Christians.

Materials

- Bibles;
- Paper and pens or pencils;
- A photocopy of the lyrics to "Stand, Fight, Win" and of the Self-Evaluation Sheet for each student;

© 1991 DKB Music/ASCAP. All rights reserved. Used by permission. Permission to photocopy granted.

- A chalkboard or overhead projector with transparencies;

Optional
- The album, *Go to the Top*, by DeGarmo and Key.

1 BEGIN

Hand out the lyrics to "Stand, Fight, Win." If you have the *Go to the Top* album, play "Stand, Fight, Win" as class members follow along with the lyrics.

Ask, **Who are DeGarmo and Key talking about when they say, "There is a ruler in the unseen world that is filled with hate"?** After a correct response (Satan or the devil), ask the class members what media portrayal of the devil seems the most accurate. This should spark some discussion about the different ways Satan is depicted in this world. Ask the students how they picture Satan. Write on the chalkboard or an overhead transparency the students' impressions.

If class members seem to have seen a lot of occult genre movies or rock groups, caution them about the unhealthy interest in the occult these days. Let them know that it is smart to be aware of the devil's schemes, but to show too much interest in the occult can be dangerous. One of the dangers is that the media does not portray all of the aspects of Satan, but only those that make a good movie. Satan's appearance can be very different from the goat-man monster usually found in film.

Read together Genesis 3:1, Isaiah 14:12 and 2 Corinthians 11:14. Discuss the implications of these verses. (Satan is subtle and crafty; he can appear to be beautiful or even as an angel.) If you have *The NIV Student Bible*, read the note concerning Isaiah 14:12. It explains the representation of Satan as the bright morning star that is eclipsed by the rising sun (representing Christ).

Optional: You may want to refer students who seem overly fearful of Satan to Romans 8:35-39 and 1 John 4:4:

Who shall separate us from the love of Christ? Shall trouble or hardship or persecution or famine or nakedness or danger or sword? As it is written: "For your sake we face death all day long; we are considered as sheep to be slaughtered." No, in all these things we are more than conquerors through him who loved us. For I am convinced that neither death nor life, neither angels nor demons, neither the present nor the future, nor any powers, neither height nor depth, nor anything else in all creation, will be able to separate us from the love of God that is in Christ Jesus our Lord. You, dear children, are from God and have overcome them, because the one who is in you is greater than the one who is in the world.

2 IT'S WAR!

Have class members turn to Ephesians 6:10-12. Ask for a volunteer to read the passage. Say, **You may recognize this famous passage as one that deals with the topic of "spiritual warfare." There's a war going on that isn't usually recognized in the physical world.** Ask students to turn to

1 Peter 5:8,9 and follow along as someone reads the passage.

Say something like, **C.S. Lewis, in The Screwtape Letters, stressed that if we envision God as the point on our ceiling where we pray, we end up limiting our belief in what God is and what He can do. If we envision Satan as a mean little guy who runs around in red pajamas, we're probably not taking his power seriously, either. It's important that we take him seriously, as long as we keep in perspective that God is the Ruler of the universe and has already defeated Satan.**

Ask, **What does the devil have to do with us? Why does he care how we act?** The answer should sound something like: The devil is in a struggle (that he can't win) for the rule of the world. When we don't act in a godly way but in a sinful way, he sees that as a battle won for his side.

Have class members move into small groups of three to four people. They are to read Romans 7:14-23 and together work out a paraphrase of the passage, writing it down. When they are finished, regather into the larger group and ask for one group to read its paraphrase. Ask, **Does anyone in this group relate to what Paul is saying in this passage?** Allow for discussion.

Say something like, **So we seem to be getting it from two angles—our own sinful nature wants to do wrong, and Satan tempts us to do wrong. Often the people we encounter, with their sinful natures and Satan pushing, want us to do wrong, too. So what's the big deal? Why don't we just give in?**

Hopefully the students will have some good reasons why we should not succumb to temptation. If they need help, or to support their answers by the Word, direct them to John 8:34,36; 14:23,24; Colossians 3:1-10; 1 Timothy 1:18,19 and 1 John 3:7-10.

3 WEAPONS FOR WARFARE

Say, **Okay, so we need to stand against temptation, we need to fight against "the powers of this dark world" that we read about in Ephesians. How do**

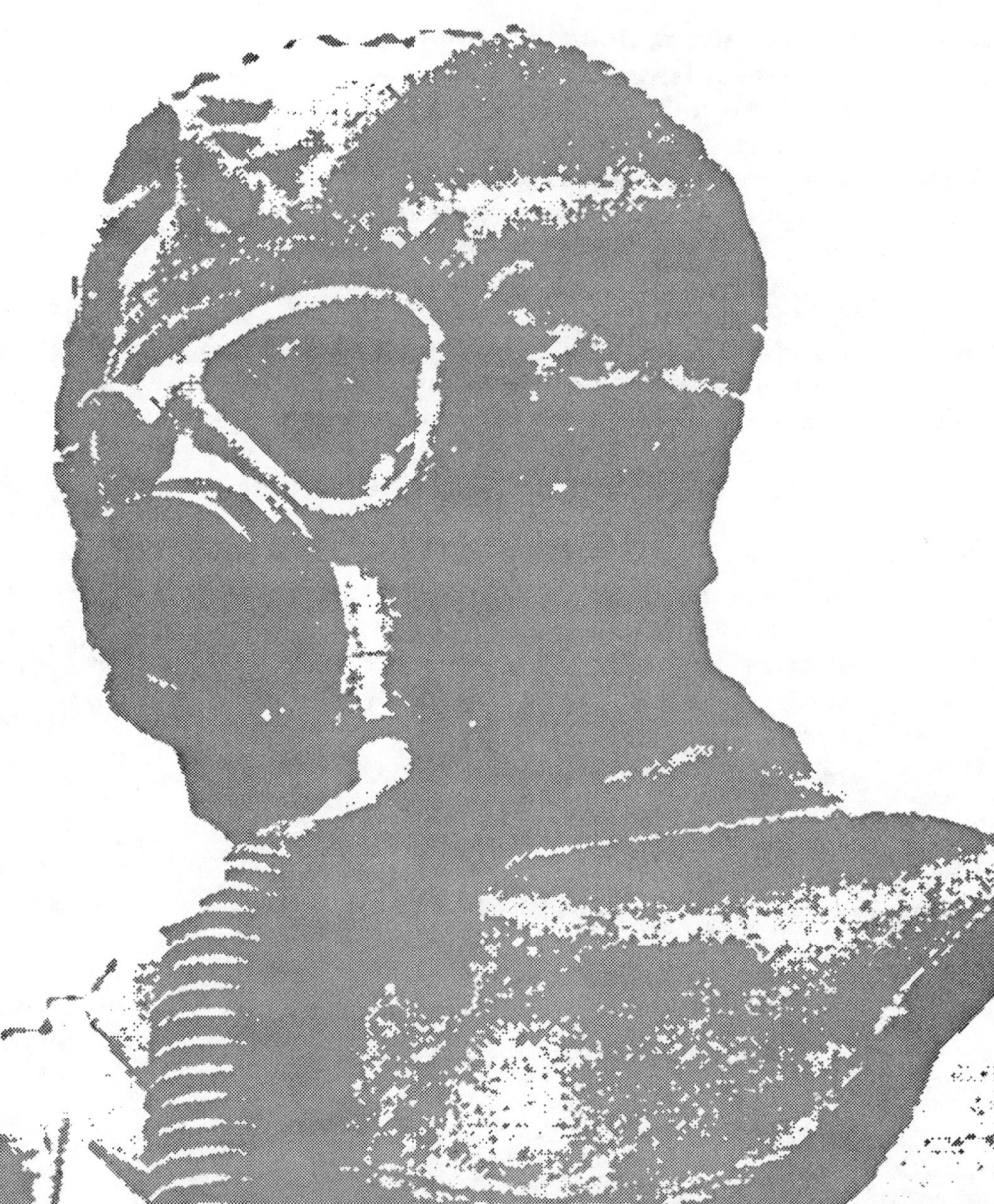

we do it? This is a rhetorical question. Don't wait for an answer. Say, **We start with Christ.** Read aloud Romans 7:24,25. Then have class members turn to Hebrews 2:18 and 4:15 and read to themselves. Ask them to tell you what they find out about how Christ can help. The points that should be covered are: Christ knows firsthand what it is like to be tempted—He can sympathize with us; He was tempted without sinning; He knows how to help us.

Have class members turn again to Ephesians 6. Ask a volunteer to read verse 13. Then ask any athletes in the room, **What do you do to get ready for competition?** You may need to prompt them with the following questions: How much time do you spend practicing? Do you wear any special clothes that help you perform well? Do you have a coach? What does your coach do? Do you eat any differently when you're in training? Do you get your mind into a certain attitude?

Then say, **Paul in this passage is acting like an assistant coach. He is telling us, "Here's what you need to wear to be ready for this fight."** Ask a volunteer to read verses 14 through 17.

Have the class divide into small groups with two to three in a group. They are to think of a sport, preferably one that requires a lot of equipment, and rewrite Ephesians 6:14-17 using this new analogy. Tell them it is important that they analyze how each piece of spiritual equipment is used, and which piece of athletic equipment might best symbolize it. When they are finished, have them regather. Each group will then share what they came up with. They may want to use one group member as the sports mannequin while another sports salesclerk tries to "sell" the class on the needed equipment.

Optional: If you have few class members interested in sports, but quite

14

a few aspiring actors, you may want to use this option. Have class members give a monologue acting as if they were a piece of spiritual armor, one actor per piece of armor. Give them a few minutes to prepare.

Ask a volunteer to read Ephesians 6:18. Repeat, **"And pray in the Spirit on all occasions with all kinds of prayers and requests."** Say, **The way Paul puts that, it makes it sound like prayer is very important in spiritual warfare. Why do you think that might be?** One good answer would be that our power against the devil comes from God. If no one comes up with that answer, say it yourself. Ask if anyone can find another verse in chapter 6 that talks about where our strength comes from. One particular verse is verse 10.

Have class members turn to Galatians 5:16-26 and take turns reading aloud. Ask them to read it silently to themselves and look for facts relative to what is being studied today. When they respond, write their answers on the chalkboard or overhead transparency. Some points you might want to bring up if they don't are: the Holy Spirit living in us is another source of power (Matt. 12:28); here is another example of the sinful nature versus the godly nature; the passage explains what happens to the sinful nature (crucified); it contains a list of acts that indicate losing the war and a list of characteristics that are indicative of winning the war.

4

WE MIGHT LOSE A BATTLE, BUT NOT THE WAR

Say, **What should we do when we lose a battle, when we mess up, when we give in to temptation?** The answer you are looking for is "confess our failure." If no one gives that answer, direct them to 1 John 1:9. If someone does give that answer, ask them where it is found in the Bible and then have everyone look it up. Another answer that may come up is that they should stop doing the sin. Direct them again to 1 John 2:4. Say, **If we really love Jesus, we need to change our ways and live like He wants us to. We'll never be able to be totally like Christ, but with God's help we should be able to become more and more Christlike.**

Have class members turn to 2 Timothy 2:3-7. If someone has *The NIV Student Bible*, have them read aloud the boxed paragraph, "Soldier, Athlete, Farmer." Then have a volunteer read the Scripture. Say, **Paul wanted Timothy to reflect on these analogies. Let's do some reflecting ourselves and see what we can come up with.** Write down any ideas they have about enduring hardship. Then say something like, **Not very many people go to war to have fun. Living for Jesus and being at war with Satan can be costly. But we look forward to a promise.** Tell the class members that you're going to give them two verses that they might want to memorize for times when they need an extra edge against the devil. Have them read James 1:12 and then 2 Timothy 4:7,8. Say, **What are we promised?** After responses, say, **Won't it feel good to be able to say at the end of our lives, "I have fought the good fight, I have finished the race, I have kept the faith"?**

If you have the album, *Go to the Top*, tell class members that you have one more exercise for them. Give them each two small pieces of paper and ask them to write down the two things that are the most tempting to them—a different one on each piece of paper. Then have them hold one of the papers in each hand. While you play "Stand, Fight, Win," they are to listen to the song and think about how it relates to the temptations they are holding in their hands. After the song is finished, as a class you may want to symbolically destroy the temptations by destroying the pieces of paper. Or suggest that the students have their own temptation-destroying ceremony at home.

Distribute the Self-Evaluation Sheets for students to work on at home.

Close in prayer.

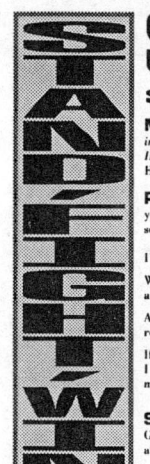

STEP 6 STAND, FIGHT, WIN
SELF-EVALUATION SHEET

Memory Verse: *Live as children of light (for the fruit of the light consists in all goodness, righteousness and truth) and find out what pleases the Lord. Have nothing to do with the fruitless deeds of darkness but rather expose them.* Ephesians 5:8-11

Personal Evaluation: Respond honestly to the statements below. Then score your responses. Use this evaluation to help you as you complete the Personal Journal section.

	Almost Always	Usually	Rarely
I fight against any temptation to sin.	☐	☐	☐
When I lose a battle against temptation and the devil, I ask God for forgiveness.	☐	☐	☐
After a situation in which I've sinned, I resist doing that sin again.	☐	☐	☐
If I am continually tempted with a sin, I ask for mature Christians to pray for me regarding that sin.	☐	☐	☐

Scoring
Give yourself three points for every "almost always" answer, one point for every "usually" and zero points for "never."
- 9-12 You are a committed disciple.
- 6-8   You are well on your way to becoming a mature, committed disciple.
- 0-5   You need to reexamine your commitment and take steps to follow through.

Personal Journal
What did you learn in this session about spiritual warfare that made you feel concerned? What did you learn that encouraged you?

Choose one temptation to sin that is the most difficult for you to resist. Make it a goal this week to daily put on your spiritual armor against this temptation, to pray daily to God about it and to stand firm.

Read again the Bible Memory Verse (see top of page). Commit it to your memory. How can you find out what pleases the Lord?

© DeGarmo and Key by Gospel Light. All rights reserved. Permission to photocopy granted.

STAND, FIGHT, WIN

Behind the news in the hearts of men
there are fights to fight and wars to win.
You've heard the trumpet sound,
this is your hour.
There is a ruler in the unseen world
that is filled with hate, filled with sin.
You've got the strength to win.
Stand in His power.

Chorus:
Stand, fight, win,
You've got the power to stand;
Stand, fight, win,
This is the hour to
Stand, fight, win.

You've got to stand and fight to win.
Don't be a slave to the mundane world;
there are fights to fight, wars to win.
Awaken from your sleep and run to the battle.
Look at your world through eyes of faith,
no time to waste, emergency.
You've got all you need,
helmet to sandal.

(chorus)

© 1991 DKB Music/ASCAP. All rights reserved. Used by permission. Permission to photocopy granted.

STEP 6 STAND, FIGHT, WIN
SELF-EVALUATION SHEET

Memory Verse: *Live as children of light (for the fruit of the light consists in all goodness, righteousness and truth) and find out what pleases the Lord. Have nothing to do with the fruitless deeds of darkness but rather expose them.* Ephesians 5:8-11

Personal Evaluation: Respond honestly to the statements below. Then score your responses. Use this evaluation to help you as you complete the Personal Journal section.

	Almost Always	Usually	Rarely
I fight against any temptation to sin.	❏	❏	❏
When I lose a battle against temptation and the devil, I ask God for forgiveness.	❏	❏	❏
After a situation in which I've sinned, I resist doing that sin again.	❏	❏	❏
If I am continually tempted with a sin, I ask for mature Christians to pray for me regarding that sin.	❏	❏	❏

Scoring
Give yourself three points for every "almost always" answer, one point for every "usually" and zero points for "rarely."

- 9-12　You are a committed disciple.
- 6-8　You are well on your way to becoming a mature, committed disciple.
- 0-5　You need to reexamine your commitment and take steps to follow through.

Personal Journal

What did you learn in this session about spiritual warfare that made you feel concerned? What did you learn that encouraged you?

Choose one temptation to sin that is the most difficult for you to resist. Make it a goal this week to daily put on your spiritual armor against this temptation, to pray daily to God about it and to stand firm.

Read again the Bible Memory Verse (see top of page). Commit it to your memory. How can you find out what pleases the Lord?

© 1991 DeGarmo and Key by Gospel Light. All rights reserved. Permission to photocopy granted.

TALK SHEET: SHINING AS STARS

Use this side of the Talk Sheet as an optional lesson outline. The reverse side of this paper may be photocopied and handed out to class members to use with the session, or if no session is planned, you may use it as a handout for the class members to take home as an additional resource to the basic lesson, Stand, Fight, Win.

Instructions

Option 1: If you use the outline as a basis for your session, add more details by doing some personal study in the Bible and other Christian books and by reflecting on what you've learned in your own life. Prepare some discussion questions (questions that cannot be answered by a simple yes or no). Use the reverse side of the Talk Sheet as a handout, resource or take-home paper.

Option 2: You may want to use only the reverse side of this page and simply lead the class members through the worksheet, clarifying points and adding any thoughts you would like.

Outline

I. Christians in society
   A. Christians are to be shining testimonies in the world (Phil. 2:14,15)
   B. Christians are to be salt and light (Matt. 5:13-26)
   C. Live responsibly (Eph. 5:15-18)

II. Christian responsibilities
   A. Called to action (Jas. 1:22; 2:14,26)
   B. Help the poor (Jas. 2:15,16)
   C. The wealthy are responsible to use wealth and power to help others (Jas. 5:1-6)
   D. To protect the powerless (Deut. 10:17,18)
   E. To "stand in the gap" (Ezek. 22:30)

III. Practical Christian activism
   A. Be informed, vote, speak up
   B. Community service
   C. Support ministries that stand for the innocent, reach the poor

IV. Optional helps
   A. "Conflicts of Rich and Poor" (see the end of the book of James in *The NIV Student Bible*)
   B. See the song "Soul Mender" from the album *Go to the Top*

© 1991 DeGarmo and Key by Gospel Light. All rights reserved. Permission to photocopy granted.

SHINING AS STARS

READ PHILIPPIANS 2:14-16.

Circle letter *A* or *B* below.
Most of the Christians I know...   A. blend in with society.   B. stand out in society like shining stars.

Write down several Scripture passages that talk about actions to do that make you stand out in society (or characteristics of godliness). If you don't know where to find them, start with the New Testament. The easiest places to look might be the Sermon on the Mount (in Matthew and Luke) and the shorter letters, such as Ephesians and Colossians. Circle a passage that you will memorize.

1.   3.

2.   4.

READ MATTHEW 5:13-16

Describe two properties of salt, comparing them to how the Christian life should be lived.

READ EPHESIANS 5:15-18

Think of three situations you were in last week and write them down: 1. 2. 3.	Write down a responsible way to act in each situation:	Write down what the irresponsible way to act would have been:

READ JAMES 1:22 AND 2:14,26

In your own words write what James is talking about.

READ JAMES 2:15,16 AND MATTHEW 25:31-46

Make a list of the types of needy people mentioned: 1. 2. 3. 4. 5.	Write down the matching thing that would fill the need:	Write down what you could do to fill that need:

Look around your community. What are some of the things you think would make the most difference in the lives of the needy people in your area?

How could you make a difference?

© 1991 DeGarmo and Key by Gospel Light. All rights reserved. Permission to photocopy granted.

There was a time when my life was empty.
There was a time when my heart grew cold.
But you came to me with a heart of mercy.
You came to me with a heart of gold.
I can't take back
the years that have passed.

Chorus:
I will give the rest of my life,
the rest of my life,
I will give the rest of my life
to you.

I loved the world and it left me lonely.
I loved myself and it left me blind.
But you came to me with a love enduring.
You came to me with a love divine.

(chorus)

(bridge)
If I could retrieve the years,
I would give them all to you,
I would give them all for you.
If I could retrieve the tears,
I would give them all to you,
I would give my all to you.

STEP 7 THE REST OF MY LIFE

Theme: Jesus wants to be Lord over every area of His disciples' lives.

Memory Verse: *Therefore, I urge you brothers, in view of God's mercy, to offer your bodies as living sacrifices, holy and pleasing to God—this is your spiritual act of worship.* Romans 12:1

Checklist

You and your students will know that you have accomplished the goals of this Bible study session if:
- ❑ Jesus is Lord of your life.
- ❑ You have submitted all areas of your life—physical, material, spiritual, emotional and social—to His control.
- ❑ Your plans for the future include plans to serve the Lord.
- ❑ As you mature as a Christian, you disciple others.

Materials
- Bibles;
- Paper and pencils or pens;
- A photocopy of the lyrics to "The Rest of My Life" and of the Self-Evaluation Sheet for each student;
- A chalkboard or overhead projector with transparencies;
- An envelope for each student;

© 1991 DKB Music/ASCAP. All rights reserved. Used by permission. Permission to photocopy granted.

Optional
- The album, *Go to the Top*, by DeGarmo and Key.
- The album, *Meet Julie Miller* or another album that contains the song, "How Could You Say No," by Mickey Cates. Another option would be any powerful song that talks about Jesus dying for us.

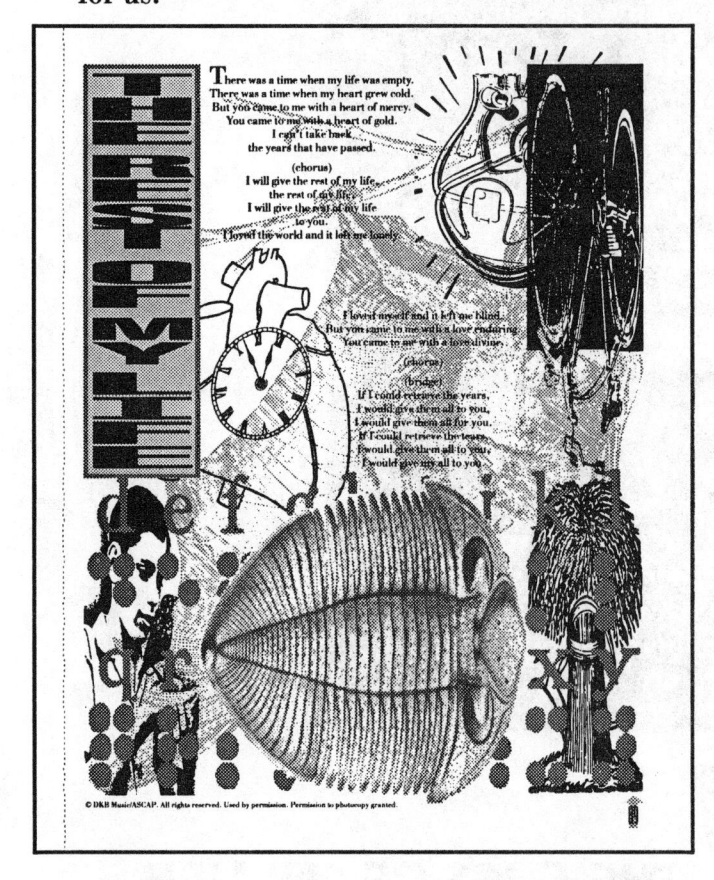

1
BEGIN

Play the song, "How Could You Say No?" or another song that talks about Jesus dying for us. Whether or not you play a song, ask the students to tell how they feel when they think about Jesus dying for them. If there is not enough response, you may want to tell about your own feelings. The purpose of all this is to set a mood that reminds class members how much Christ has done for them and how much they owe the Lord (their lives).

Have class members turn to 2 Corinthians 5:15. Ask for a volunteer to read. Then ask if this verse reminds anybody of a song lyric from DeGarmo and Key. What it might remind them of is the line from "The Pledge" (from the album *The Pledge*), "He died for me, I'll live for Him."

Say something like, **During the last six (11 or however many sessions you've taught) sessions, I hope you've gotten a good idea of what it means to live for Christ—what actions to take and what attitudes to have. Today I want to emphasize that when you live for Jesus, that means every part of your life is His.**

2
LORD OF ALL

Hand out a piece of paper and a pencil to each class member. Ask them to make two columns. In the left column, they are to brainstorm and write down every single area of their lives that they can think of. That includes every relationship, every activity, every dream, every thought. Give them about five minutes to write. When they are finished writing, give the following instructions on what they are to write in the right-hand column: They are to grade themselves and write comments about how well they are doing at living for Jesus in each area of their lives listed. You will want to give them plenty of time to do this. If some take a lot longer than others, suggest that they finish at home.

Ask, **Did any of you learn something from this exercise that you would like to share with the group?** Allow time for discussion.

3
HIS HANDS AND FEET

Say something like, **There's an idiom that's used a lot in Christian circles about how we live for Jesus—it's often called "being God's hands and feet." A similar example to this was used by Randy Stonehill in his song, "Who Will Save the Children?" That phrase was about being God's hands and voice for hungry and homeless children.** Ask if class members can think of any other ways this kind of symbolism has been used in Christian literature, music or visual art. Use these ideas to get them started: the painting by Dürer of the praying hands; the cover of Tony Campolo's book, *Ideas for Social Action* that shows a hand holding out a cup of water.

Have class members turn to Isaiah 52:7. After a volunteer reads, say, **Here's another example—feet equated with the bringing of good news. Handel used this verse in "The Messiah."** Ask class members to turn to Romans 10:14,15. Have a volunteer read the passage. Say, **Paul picked up this "beautiful feet" phrase and used it to talk about spreading the good**

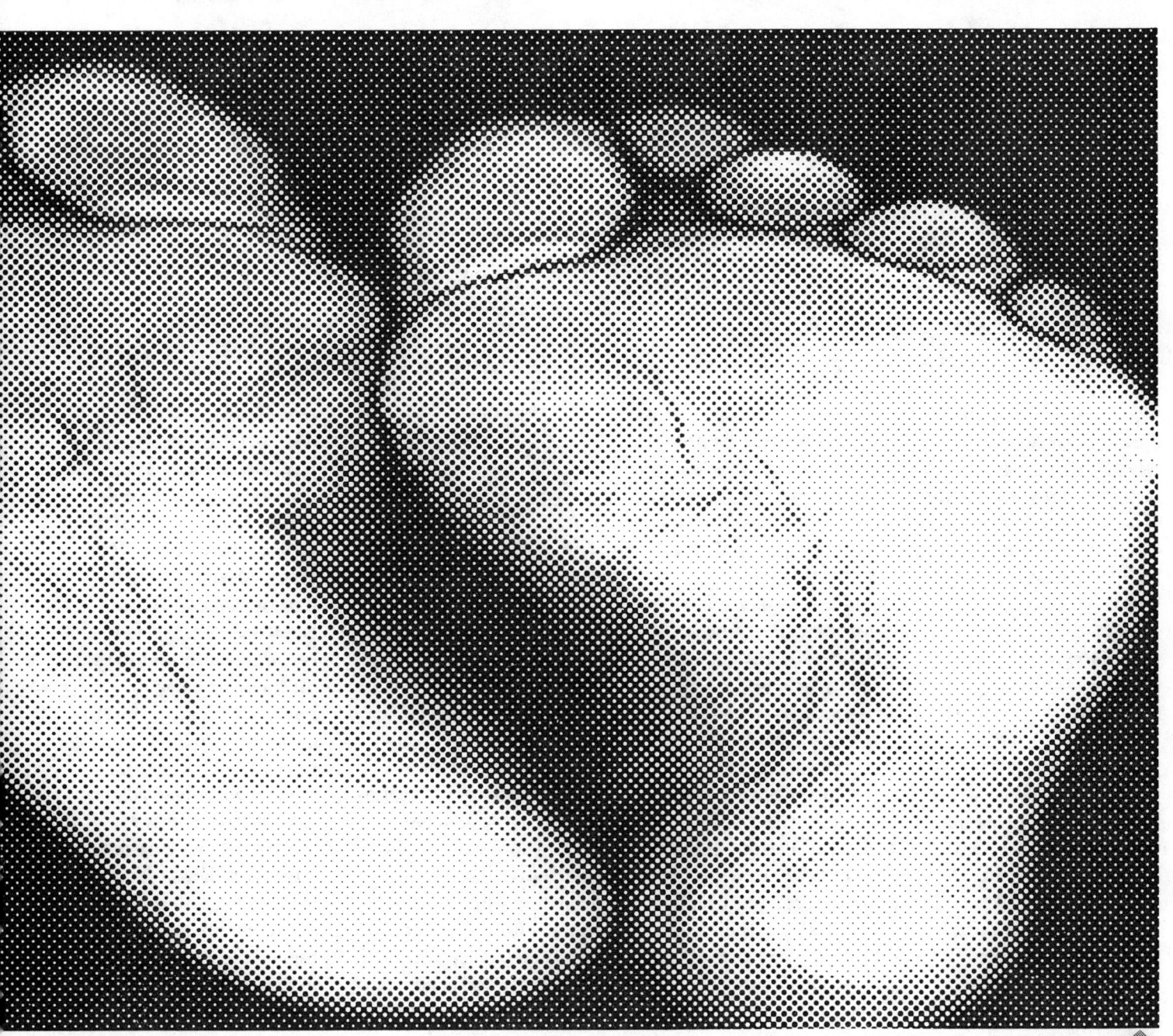

news about Christ. Telling others about Jesus is a major way of being God's hands and feet. Ask, **What might be some others?**

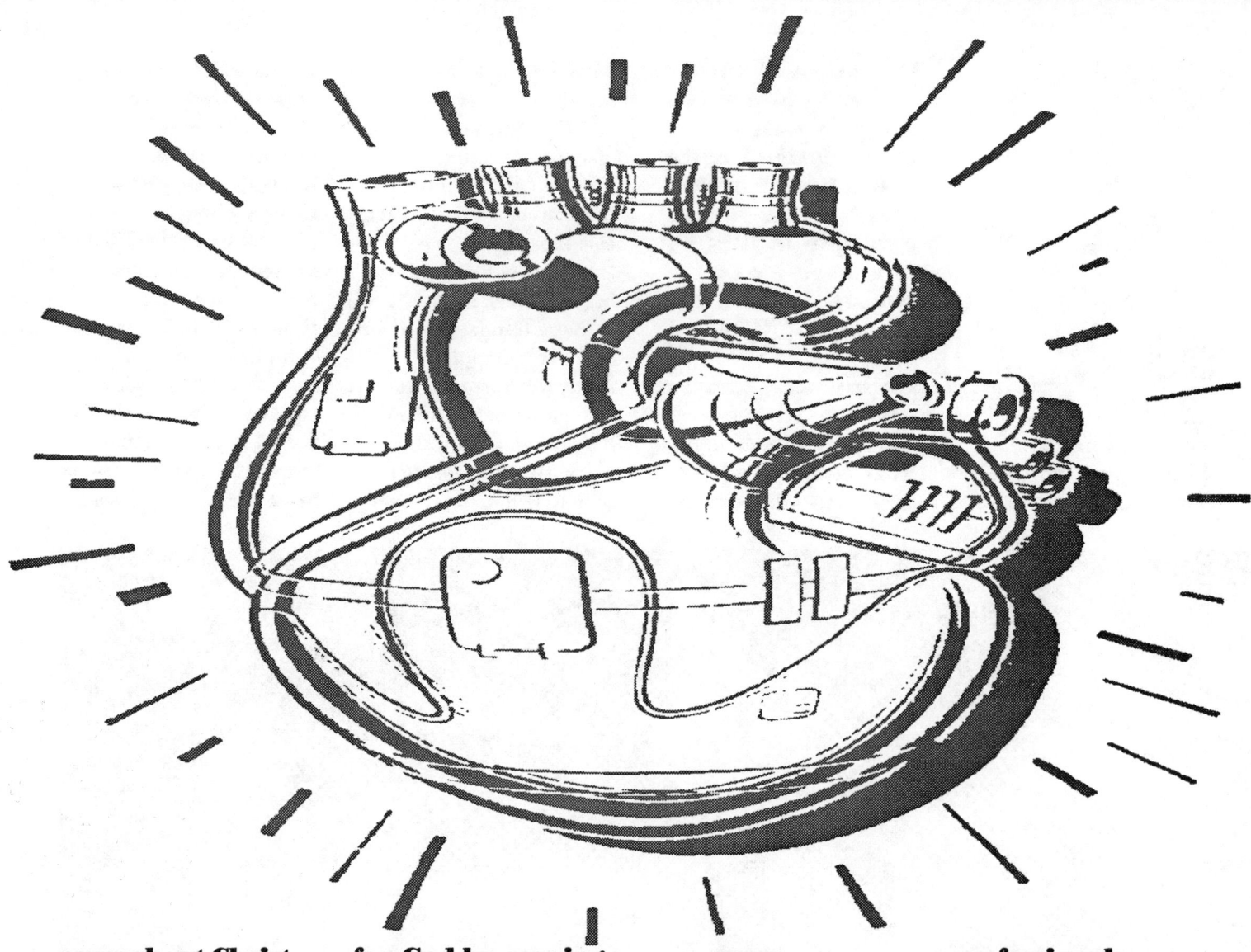

Write on a chalkboard or overhead transparency the responses that are given. Then have the students turn to Matthew 25:34-40 and have three volunteers read. (One as narrator, one as the King, one as the righteous.) Say something like, **There's an extra dimension here. Not only are the righteous working for God by serving others, but Jesus says they are actually serving Jesus.** Add, **Mother Teresa takes this quite literally. She says that when she serves and looks into the faces of the poorest of the poor, she sees the face of Jesus.** You might want to ask if anyone in the class has ever worked with the very poor. If anyone has, ask them to share what the faces of the poor look like. Ask for their reflection on what Jesus being "the least of these" means to them.

4 VOCATION AND AVOCATION

Say, **Another word for serving is "ministering."** If some responses on the chalkboard are about being ministers, direct attention to those responses. Say something like, **Some people are called to be church professionals, sometimes called "ministers." But every Christian is called to be a minister of reconciliation. Does anyone know what that means?** Write down responses and points that hit home or close to home. Then have the students turn to 2 Corinthians 5:17-20. After a volunteer reads, ask, **What does it mean to be reconciled to God?** You're looking for an answer along the lines of restoring your relationship with God (which is done through Christ). Say, **So**

being a minister of reconciliation means—Let the class members fill in the blank. Remind them that this is every Christian's job description.

Then say, **Some of you may be called to be full-time and/or professional ministers. Let's make a list of what kind of ministers that could include.** Write down their responses on a chalkboard or overhead transparency as they call them out. The list should include: pastor, youth minister, music minister, administrator, missionary, church secretary, Christian education director, Christian service worker, Christian media worker. Ask the students to turn to 1 Peter 2:9. After a volunteer reads, say, **Some theologians talk about "the priesthood of all believers." The practical philosophy here is that the work of ministry should not be limited to the pros—the pastors' main job should be to equip the congregation to do the work of the ministry.**

Say something like, **Whether or not you are called to church work as your vocation, everyone is called to function in some role in the Body of Christ.** Direct class members' attention to 1 Corinthians 12:27,28 and have a volunteer read. Ask for examples of how people in your church serve. Then inquire if any of the class members are interested in a certain church role, but aren't sure how to fulfill it. Discuss different ways to serve in the church as a volunteer. Direct students who want to serve in the church to people who can get them involved.

5

MAKING DISCIPLES

Have class members turn to Matthew 28:18-20. Brief the class on

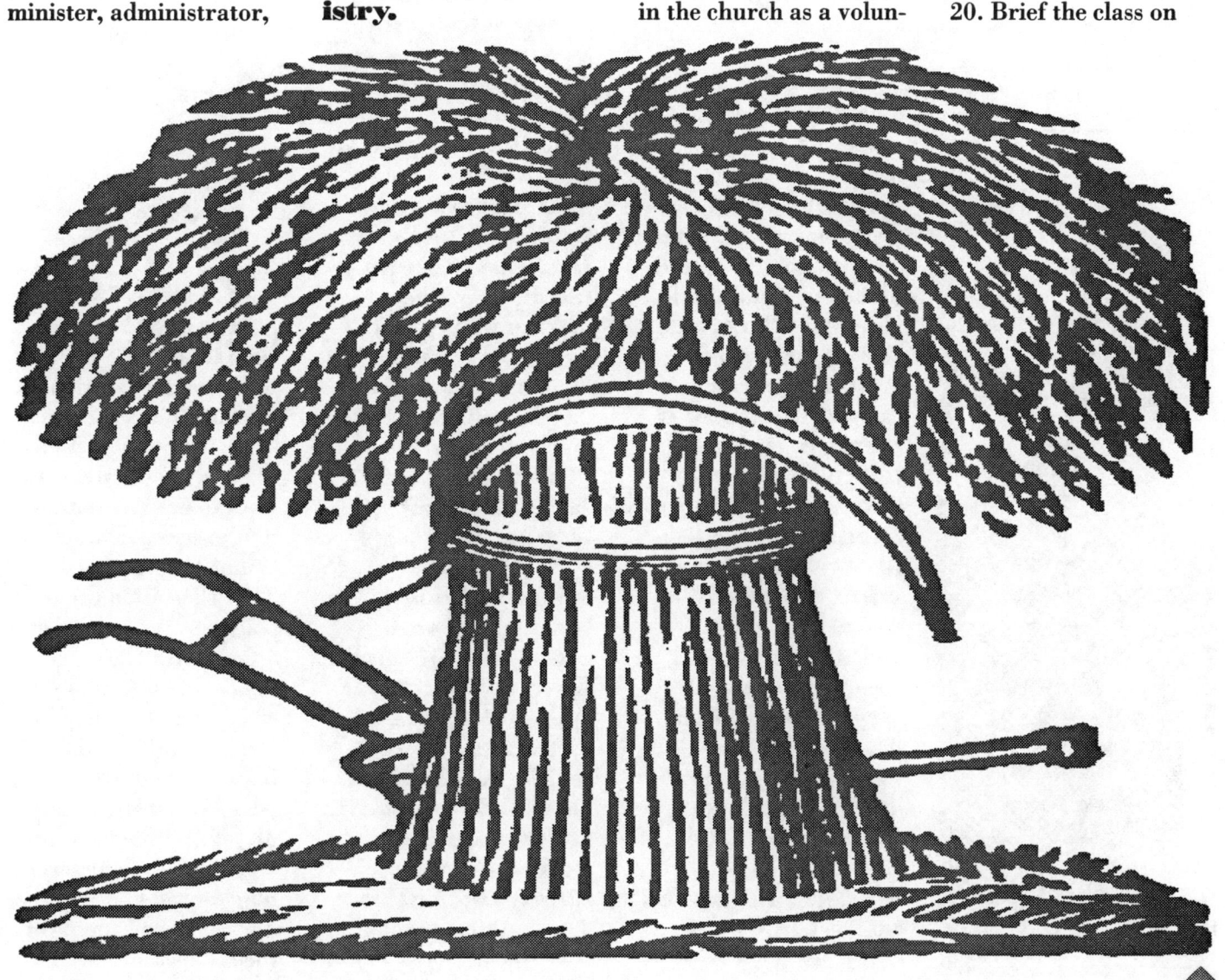

STEP 7 — THE REST OF MY LIFE
SELF-EVALUATION SHEET

Memory Verse: Therefore, I urge you brothers, in view of God's mercy, to offer your bodies as living sacrifices, holy and pleasing to God—this is your spiritual act of worship. Romans 12:1

Personal Evaluation: Respond honestly to the statements below. Then score your responses. Use this evaluation to help you as you complete the Personal Journal.

	Almost Always	Usually	Rarely
I submit every area of my life to God's control.	❑	❑	❑
I tell other people about the good news of Jesus.	❑	❑	❑
My plans for the future include plans to serve the Lord.	❑	❑	❑
As I mature as a Christian, I disciple others for Christ.	❑	❑	❑

Scoring
Give yourself three points for every "almost always" answer, one point for every "usually" and zero points for "never."
- 9-12 You are a committed disciple.
- 6-8 You are well on your way to becoming a mature, committed disciple.
- 0-5 You need to reexamine your commitment and take steps to follow through.

Personal Journal
What insight did you gain from this session about the possibilities for your future?

What specific area of your life will you single out this week to give wholeheartedly to the Lord's control?

Read again the Bible Memory Verse (see top of page). Commit it to your memory. What do you think it means to "offer your bodies as living sacrifices"?

How can your life be more holy and pleasing to God?

© DeGarmo and Key by Gospel Light. All rights reserved. Permission to photocopy granted.

---

what is happening at this point in the Scripture (Jesus has risen from the dead and has appeared to the remaining disciples). Ask, **What are Jesus' instructions?** After responses, ask, **What would it mean to a disciple to "go and make disciples"? They should have a pretty good idea what a disciple is, shouldn't they?** Talk about how Jesus spent most of His ministry working with His disciples—the whole time He was giving them an example of how they were to act when He was gone. Say something like, **We don't spend our whole lives only being disciples. When we reach a certain amount of maturity in our faith, it is only natural that we begin to disciple others.** Ask class members what they think this might mean.

Say, **This is a very important time in your life—soon, if you're not already, you'll be making decisions about how you're going to spend the rest of your life.** Have them turn over the paper they used for listing all the areas in their lives. Say, **Write down what some of your plans for the future are.** After a few minutes, say, **Now I want you to think about how you can serve God. Don't leave Him out of your plans.** Have them make any notes they want to on the subject.

Hand out another piece of paper, an envelope and the lyrics to "The Rest of My Life" to each student. Say, **During this song, I'd like you to write out some kind of commitment to God about how you will spend the rest of your life. You might want to tell God how you will serve Him, or your feelings about the future.** Then tell them that after they finish, they will put their papers in the envelopes with their addresses, seal them and give them to you. In six months or a year, you will mail the envelopes to the class.

Optional: Play the song, "The Rest of My Life."

After the class members have finished writing, collect their envelopes.

Distribute the Self-Evaluation Sheet for students to work on at home.

Close in prayer.

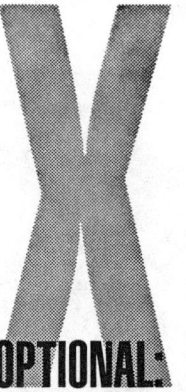

OPTIONAL:

Following this session, or session 13 if you are using the optional Talk Sheet sessions, you may want to have a celebration to commemorate completing the course. The celebration could feature refreshments and a time when class members could informally share what they have learned and how they have grown during the past few weeks of study. To set the mood and provide discussion material, play the video, *Go to the Top*, at the beginning of the celebration.

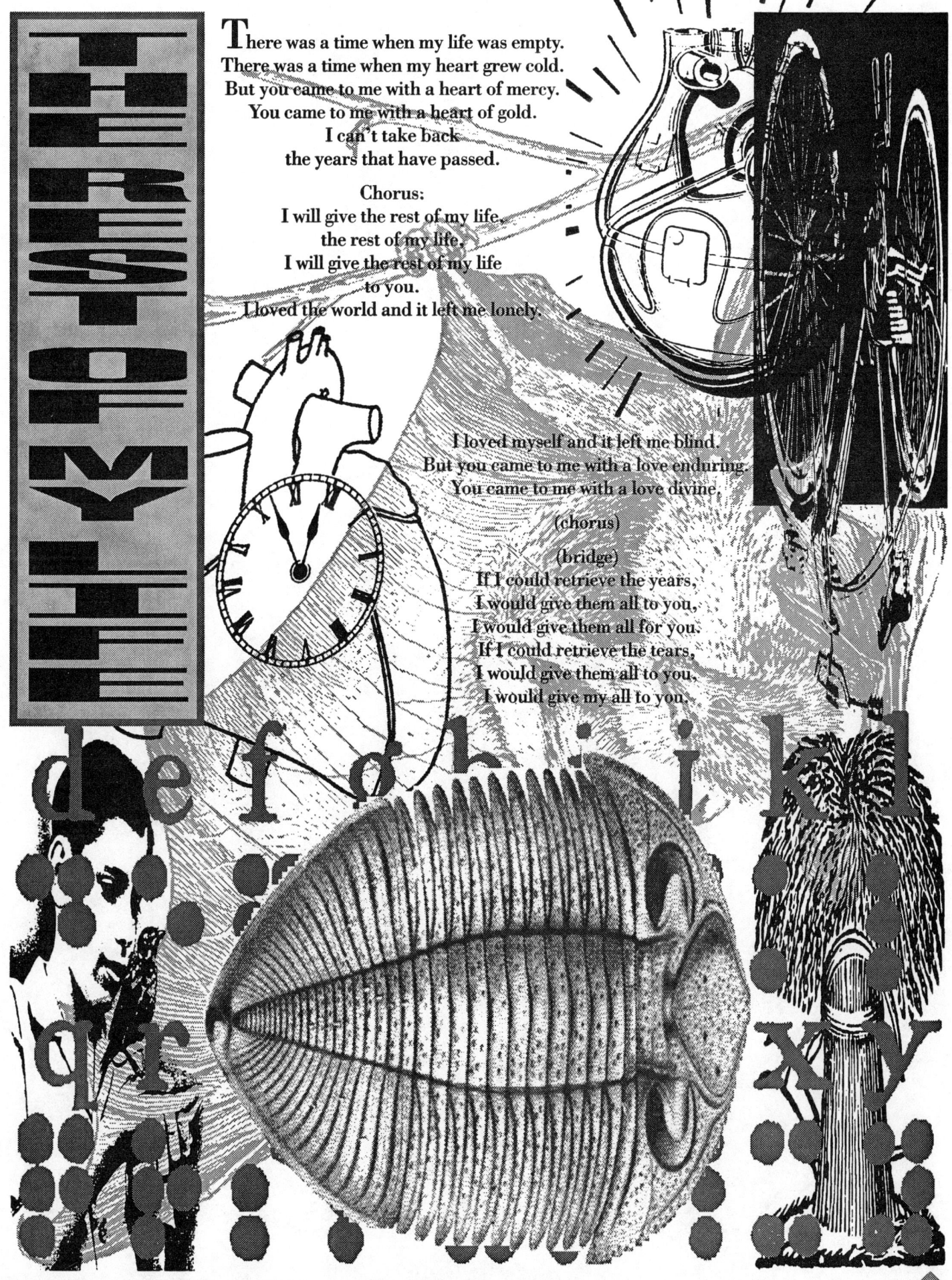

THE REST OF MY LIFE

There was a time when my life was empty.
There was a time when my heart grew cold.
But you came to me with a heart of mercy.
You came to me with a heart of gold.
I can't take back
the years that have passed.

Chorus:
I will give the rest of my life,
the rest of my life,
I will give the rest of my life
to you.
I loved the world and it left me lonely.
I loved myself and it left me blind.
But you came to me with a love enduring.
You came to me with a love divine.

(chorus)

(bridge)
If I could retrieve the years,
I would give them all to you,
I would give them all for you.
If I could retrieve the tears,
I would give them all to you,
I would give my all to you.

© 1991 DKB Music/ASCAP. All rights reserved. Used by permission. Permission to photocopy granted.

STEP 7 THE REST OF MY LIFE
SELF-EVALUATION SHEET

Memory Verse: *Therefore, I urge you brothers, in view of God's mercy, to offer your bodies as living sacrifices, holy and pleasing to God—this is your spiritual act of worship.* Romans 12:1

Personal Evaluation: Respond honestly to the statements below. Then score your responses. Use this evaluation to help you as you complete the Personal Journal.

	Almost Always	Usually	Rarely
I submit every area of my life to God's control.	❑	❑	❑
I tell other people about the good news of Jesus.	❑	❑	❑
My plans for the future include plans to serve the Lord.	❑	❑	❑
As I mature as a Christian, I disciple others for Christ.	❑	❑	❑

Scoring
Give yourself three points for every "almost always" answer, one point for every "usually" and zero points for "rarely."

- 9-12   You are a committed disciple.
- 6-8   You are well on your way to becoming a mature, committed disciple.
- 0-5   You need to reexamine your commitment and take steps to follow through.

Personal Journal
What insight did you gain from this session about the possibilities for your future?

What specific area of your life will you single out this week to give wholeheartedly to the Lord's control?

Read again the Bible Memory Verse (see top of page). Commit it to your memory. What do you think it means to "offer your bodies as living sacrifices"?

How can your life be more holy and pleasing to God?

© 1991 DeGarmo and Key by Gospel Light. All rights reserved. Permission to photocopy granted.

TALK SHEET: YOUR PERSONAL TESTIMONY

Use this side of the Talk Sheet as an optional lesson outline. The reverse side of this paper may be photocopied and handed out to class members to use with the session, or if no session is planned, you may use it as a handout for class members to take home as an additional resource for the Step 7 session.

Instructions

Option 1: If you use the outline as a basis for your session, add more details by doing some personal study in the Bible and other Christian books and by reflecting on what you've learned in your own life. Prepare some discussion questions (questions that cannot be answered by a simple yes or no). Use the reverse side of the Talk Sheet as a handout, resource or take-home paper.

Option 2: You may want to use only the reverse side of this page and simply lead the class members through the worksheet, clarifying points and adding any thoughts you would like.

Outline

I. Witness—Someone who tells about his or her experience with Christ
   A. Example: John (1 John 1:1-3)
   B. Need not be a pastor or theologian. Simply tell others how Jesus loved and saved you and what He has done in your life.
   C. The sacrifice of a witness: must care more about the world's opinion of Jesus than its opinion of you.

II. You are commanded to witness (Matt. 28:19,20; Acts 1:8; 1 Pet. 2:9)

III. You are competent to witness
   A. Have the Holy Spirit
   B. Have your testimony

IV. Prepare your personal testimony: two models
   A. Chronological (going through the events of your life)

   Before   conversion   after

   B. Thematic (relating how conversion affected a problem in your life)

   Now   conversion   after
   (begin with a problem)

© 1991 DeGarmo and Key by Gospel Light. All rights reserved. Permission to photocopy granted.

YOUR PERSONAL TESTIMONY

Look up a dictionary definition of a witness and write down your paraphrase here:	Look up 1 John 1:1-4 and write down any key facts about what it is to be a Christian witness:	Fill in the blanks: A witness must care more about the world's _____ of Jesus than its opinion of _____.
Look up Matthew 28:19,20. Write down all the action words in this column.	Look up Acts 1:8. What new element is present in this verse?	Look up 1 Peter 2:9. How is witnessing described here?

Life-style evangelism is living in such a way as to make people ask, "Why do you live this way? What makes you different from other people?" Such queries provide an excellent opportunity to tell others how Jesus changed your life.

In this column, write down situations that you were in during the last month where you could have been a better witness through your life-style? How?

In this column, write down circumstances that may come up in the next month where you can plan to be a better witness through your life-style. How?

Below are some examples of other ways and opportunities to witness. Add your own, and make a mark beside those you would consider doing.

___ write a song and sing it
___ write a story and let people read it
___ write a letter to someone
___ put together and display a photo essay

___ use a speech assignment to talk about Christ
___ other:_____
_____
_____

Answer the following questions to help you prepare your personal testimony:

1. How has Christ changed my life?

2. What might I be like if I didn't have Christ?

3. What special things has Christ done for me?

4. How have Christ's love, strength and support been made visible in my life?

5. What might life be like without Christ?

© 1991 DeGarmo and Key by Gospel Light. All rights reserved. Permission to photocopy granted.

TEACHING/LEARNING TOOLS
for use with your basic text, the Bible

Skitsophrenia is full of skits that teach Bible truths in an entertaining way. It also has skits for announcing events during a worship service or youth group meeting, skits to use for evangelization and articles on the art of presenting skits and how they may be used to build up the Body of Christ.

So, What's a Christian Anyway? is a fun and simple way to explain salvation and the basics of Christianity to youth. It contains articles and games on how to use the Bible, belief, prayer, commitment and more. Order one for each of your students.

Outrageous Object Lessons will rivet your students' attention on the truth of God's Word. Contains over forty object lessons, each with tips and related Bible passages.

Pioneer Crafts for Kids is an illustrated craft and activity book. Includes a youth section containing 10 challenging craft ideas.

How to Do Bible Learning Activities, Grades 7-12 (Volumes 1 & 2) have complete step-by-step instructions for a wide range of learning activities to supplement any teacher's manual. Order one for every teacher.

Getting Ready for the Guy/Girl Thing is a fun new book from Focus on the Family Youth Editors Greg Johnson and Susie Shellenberger which includes God's plan for 10- to 15-year-olds on how to relate to the opposite sex. Contains discussion starter questions, quizzes, fun Q&A sections, inside scoop from Greg and Susie, great graphics, and an upbeat creative and Bible-based message for junior highers as they enter the dating years.

A Shadow of a Man (for boys only!). A timely and flexible course aimed at young teenage boys. Contrasts the illusion of manhood the world presents with the reality of godly manhood and maturity Christ modeled.

The Complete Junior High Bible Study Resource Books #1-#12 are complete, all-in-one books that contain everything a leader needs to teach any size group of junior high students about the basics of Christianity. Each manual includes 13 teacher's Bible studies and session plans; reproducible student worksheets and take-home papers; 13 midweek Bible study outlines; dozens of action games; and a section of clip art.

The Youth Worker's Emergency Manual contains tons of great ideas, activities, games and Bible studies that you can use with just minutes' notice! Special articles on how to avoid emergencies and how to create a "prop box" help youth workers run their ministries with professionalism.

101 Outrageous Things to Do with a Video Camera gives offbeat fun and easy ideas for using this new medium with your youth group.

The Incredible Fun Book! with its great games, stories and puzzles can add an element of fun to many situations. This book will provide hours of brain-teasing, incredible fun and also a chance to learn valuable truths about God, Jesus, the Bible and the basics of being a Christian.

The Youth Worker's Clip Art Book, The Youth Worker's Son of Clip Art Book, I Was a Teenage Clip Art Book and **The Complete Bible Story Clip Art Book** all contain fresh, all-new illustrations for you to clip out and arrange to create mail outs, posters, flyers, calendars, hand outs and more.

Preparing for Adolescence, by Dr. James Dobson, speaks frankly and openly to adolescents, parents and leaders about the difficult teenage years. Dr. Dobson candidly discusses the topics that trouble young teenagers most.